T0194245

Walking Tall:
Poems for Life

The Revised Edition

SEAN S. JOHN

WESTBOW
PRESS®
A DIVISION OF THOMAS NELSON
& ZONDERVAN

Home Telephone: (784)-496-3663
WhatsApp: (869)-668-4410
Facebook: Johnsilver
Email: seanjohnsilver71@outlook.com

WestBow Press books may be ordered through booksellers or by contacting:

WestBow Press
A Division of Thomas Nelson & Zondervan
1663 Liberty Drive
Bloomington, IN 47403
www.westbowpress.com
1 (866) 928-1240

ISBN: 978-1-9736-3075-3 (sc)
ISBN: 978-1-9736-3074-6 (hc)
ISBN: 978-1-9736-3076-0 (e)

Library of Congress Control Number: 2018906928

Print information available on the last page.

WestBow Press rev. date: 06/28/2018

Contents

Acknowledgments

I am obligated to express my gratitude to the Almighty God for blessing me with the favor to complete this project. I am grateful for the gift and for the privilege and opportunity to share it with others. I am especially grateful for the journey and the challenges encountered along the way. But it is finished, and I am particularly excited just because. If only words were able to fully express such gratitude!

To Anotinetta, Nevilla, Fiona, and those who prefer to remain unnamed, I thank you all for your support and encouragement, and for the initial push. Your support has encouraged me to encourage and empower myself, and I am blessed to have you as friends.

To you, the reader, I express my thanks to you for supporting this effort. I consider this a labor of love, and I hope you enjoy reading this material as much as I enjoyed writing it. And that it may bring you some measure of pleasure as you invest your time reading this book.

Dedication

To Mr. J. Calvin Fahie, Yvonne Fahie, and the extended family, this is an open expression of my gratitude to you for opening the warmth of your hearts to me and the comfort of your home when I was in need and searching for myself. Thank you for embracing me as one of your own and treating me as an equal. I am forever grateful for your love and support.

You have not spared anything good from me, and it is my prayer that, in like manner, so the Lord will not spare anything good from you, and that your investment in my development is rewarded accordingly. As you are being blessed, it is my hope that at least one other is also being blessed through you.

Preface

From the onset, this journey would prove to be more challenging than anticipated. I thought it would not be as difficult as it turned out to be. Considering that I was about to undergo the exercise of reproducing my own original work, it should have been somewhat a breeze of an exercise. But I couldn't be more wrong! This was no Sunday afternoon walk on the beach, and I was about to learn the hard way. There were long, tiring days and countless sleepless nights. There were times I actually felt like giving up. This journey required a different approach to discipline, willpower, and commitment. I was pushed to limits beyond where I had ever gone before. And although I made a conscious decision for the undertaking, as I progressed, I began to question the very rationale of that decision. It was almost like a self-inflicted injury at the beginning, and I had only myself to blame. No one had asked me to do it, but there was this still, small voice echoing time and again in my head of the need to consider the exercise. Notwithstanding, aside from the inner voice pounding on me, it was something I had entertained a few years earlier, shortly after the publication of the initial project. I guess I was simply trying to avoid the inevitable and obvious.

Walking Tall: Poems for Life—The Revised Edition is a reproduction of the original collection, first published in 2009. The decision to reproduce an updated and revised version stemmed from a sense of dissatisfaction of the quality of material produced initially, which came about after careful review and analysis of the finished product. I considered this exercise the privilege of a second chance to make a first impression, if ever that can occur. The initial approach, mind-set and energy were all wrong, and as such, I fell short of the mark. There was no shortage of support and encouragement then. In fact, I embarked on the exercise then to satisfy the number of people pushing me to publish. It would have appeared they demonstrated greater confidence in me and my abilities than I did myself. But it seemed like the right thing to do at the time. I went ahead full steam, but all of me wasn't into it. I concentrated more on quantity at the expense of quality, and preparation and planning were sacrificed for speed. I had established a deadline to completion, despite the fact there was no rush. It all started out wrong, and because there was no intervention, the outcome was disappointing to say the least, but not surprising.

Experience taught me that once started wrong, it will end that way if there is no intervention, and this was no exception. Although the outcome was disappointing, I was not disappointed. I had foreseen it, and as such, my mind was settled. In fact, I was somewhat encouraged and empowered, and invested the requisite time and thought into the next step, intending on not repeating similar mistakes and attitudes of the past.

For this project to be the success I intended, I had to change my mind-set. And so I did! Success for me simply meant producing a product I was pleased with—that I would be satisfied with—because of the quality of effort and commitment put into it from the beginning. It required a new attitude, approach, mind-set, preparation, and planning. I had to restructure me, and I rose to the occasion. Granted, it was only when I began the process that I understood how much was needed. But I became a fast learner and positioned myself for the challenge of the task ahead. This time, there was no restricting deadlines, and speed was curtailed, producing a satisfactory product, which was the goal. And to ensure that I was settled on the individual title, I dedicated time to continuous review and analysis to satisfy myself that each poem delivered the message I intended. By this time, I was already retired, and since I had no immediate or pressing obligations to contend with, I had as much time at my disposal as I was privileged to enjoy. And I was prepared not to waste a minute of it on any given day.

I armed myself with the required attitude of mind and intent, and the approach was with purpose and goal. Day by day, as it progressed, and despite the challenging moments—at times I even contemplated forgoing an individual title for an easier one because it proved too difficult—I stuck with it. Several times along the way, I had to change my mind to address particular situations. But I did not give up or consider giving up simply because it appeared difficult from time to time. By constantly changing my mind to meet the challenge encountered, I was able to overcome and complete the journey to a standard and quality as intended. And I couldn't be more pleased and satisfied!

I have realized real growth along this journey, and I am more than satisfied and content with the result. I have come to learn more about me, and the more I observed, the greater my curiosity grew. It made me more aware as well of the human spirit and the will to win. I admit there were times when I surprised myself at the level of commitment, dedication, discipline, and attitude I developed along the way and used to complete this project. This was indeed a labor of love, and I am pleased with myself.

It is my hope at least one title in this compilation will positively impact those who are privileged and have the opportunity to invest a moment of their time in the pages of this publication. I am excited to have put together this selection of poems, and I hope each reader enjoys reading them as much as I enjoyed putting them together. This is by no means the end of the road for me; I am already at an advanced stage with my next project. This is seemingly life's gift to me, and I intend to exercise it to the best of my ability and for the benefit and upliftment of as many as will have access. I am delighted to have this special gift and the privilege to share it with you.

I am grateful for your support. I challenge each of you to keep walking tall. Or if you haven't, challenge yourself to do so. Happy reading until we meet again!

Greatness

Greatness! It passes me by every day.
Occasionally, I was an obstacle in its way.
Then I was unwittingly a stumbling block.
Then my very presence was holding it back.
Once a mind shows reluctance to heal itself first,
Any forced attempts of entry may even be worse.
Had the spirit of my mind not been renewed,
I may not have known greatness was an attitude,
That greatness is the attitude of the mind!
That it is not an achievement but a way of life,
Having little to do with the power of imagination.
It is a culture of thought, a learned inclination.
Greatness is the consciousness of choice!
The decision to be silent or silence the noise
That feeds the mind or resides within.
Greatness is a living and breathing organism.
Be it the will to confront that challenge, dare,
Or be one's own worst enemy or greatest fear.
Notwithstanding, it is a calculated act of will
To decide to become active or simply stand still,
To conform to set limits or go beyond the line.
Greatness! It is essentially a state of mind,
An awareness of the power of choice in hand.
Yet a fixed reluctance to make a decisive stand,
To become self-restricted, averse to thinking anew.
Greatness is what the mind has behaved itself into
The will to cultivate the seeds of expectation of growth,
Or do nothing while the fields of potential slowly choke.
One mind's agony of defeat is another's thrill of victory,
While one's thrill of victory is another mind's injury.

Indeed, a mind may be a terrible thing to waste.
But it is always at its greatest in its settled place.
Greatness takes firm discipline, a lifetime to build.
Be it growth or stagnation, it is a question of will,
Ever-dueling rivals in a constant bid for control.
The mind—the battleground—is the ultimate goal,
To surrender to fear or seize that moment in time.
Greatness is not a triumph; it is a state of mind.

A Cry for Help

I am like a runaway train, off course and on the wrong track.
I am quickly losing control and have difficulty pulling it back.
I am on a collision course; there is imminent danger on the line.
At the rate at which I am going, the end could come anytime.
Without a timely intervention, if no real solution is soon found,
A tragedy with disastrous consequences would be the outcome.

There is a conflict of voices in my head, taunting me as I go.
They represent a real challenge to distinguish friend from foe.
The confusion is disruptive; the pressure increases, overwhelms.
My attempt to correct it on my own pushes me to another realm.
My mind is deeply corrupted; without help, I can barely stand.
I am in the fight of my life, desperate, and need a helping hand.

Doubt is beginning to consume me; I question even who I am.
I struggle to determine if I am a machine or if I am still a man.
For in this intense battle of wills, I am gradually losing control.
The evils that corrupted me enjoy a commanding hold.
I am up against great odds in this mounting battle for my mind.
Defeat seems all but certain if I don't get the help I need in time.

The evils that surround me are relentless—a compelling force.
Broken and without a sense of direction, I fight to stay the course.
As if I am having a terrible dream, I wish I would soon wake up.
At the rate at which I am going, in an instant, I could self-destruct.
I am fast approaching the dividing line, the point of no return.
I need help saving me from myself, or else I will crash and burn.

Victory seems an elusive thrill as I confront the agony of defeat.
As many attempts to claim it; as many times it withdraws in retreat.
Just when I thought I was making real strides, that I recovered it all,
I lose my sense of balance and then another fall.
The great intensity of the battle! It is simply too much to have to tell!
I am on a collision course; it is a battle for my life, me against myself.

I am lost and misdirected, and at the expense of my sense of place,
In part by external influences, and in part by the error of my ways.
The evils that invaded my mind, they fed off my innocence,
And at a time when I was impressionable, no safety net for defense.
It is seemingly an ever-mounting battle, agonizing and quite intense.
This is the ultimate fight for my life; a battle to save me from myself.

A Fear of the Heart

It is evident that you can never die!
You are a gust of wind blowing by,
As unrelenting as breaking waves.
A beast that could never be caged.
A ghostly figure, a malignant bliss,
Though only in the mind do you exist.
An attentive ear for that rabid call.
A comforter for those who may fall.

Daily you enjoy long, solitary walks.
You roam aimlessly along life's paths,
Bearing no specific intention in mind,
No sinister purpose, or evils by design.
But your name is frightening; it scares.
Vexing by nature, they call you, "Fear!"
They say you make a mind lose its will.
That when present, courage stands still.

Many consider you as the evil landed.
So I decided to get an understanding.
But so as to get an appreciation of you,
I needed to change my mind in order to.
I had to do it all from behind the scenes.
So it became a part of my daily routine.
With each passing day, a balancing act.
But it wouldn't be for long, the eerie fact!

The depth of that which I uncovered!
A telling discovery, yet I felt empowered.
The truth that unfolded opened my eyes.
I was encouraged as a result of the exercise.
An inconspicuous figure in its own space,
Just out and about with no sense of place.
A whisper of a voice, a reserved disposition,
But a guarded secret I had never envisioned.

They embrace you as a comforting friend!
Be it an avenue of escape or means to an end,
Many find refuge in you when they lack will.
And by being obedient in nature, you fulfill.
But I uncovered what was previously unknown.
Like humans, you do possess fears of your own.
One's most valued asset, that which sets one apart,
Like humans do, you, too, have a fear of the heart.

The heart is one's center and foundation.
It tells about who one is, every inclination.
One's strengths and weaknesses at one's core.
It is where our most valued assets are stored.
One can only break against oneself.
Self-preservation is key above everything else.
One's heart is the gateway to the soul.
Imagine the outcome should one lose control!

By studying you closely, I would soon discover
That you by yourself hold no enduring power.
In fact, you only have power to accommodate.
Your power is only reactive in its natural state.
Once the will of the mind and courage combine,
You become a stepping-stone on which to climb.
Fear, it's not you that humans fear most as thought.
One's greatest of all fears is fear of the heart.

A New Day

The birth of a new dawn!
It tells that a new day is born.
Daylight chases the darkness away,
And as the darkness retreats,
Life gradually rises from its sleep
And embraces the light of a new day.

A new day has come!
It forms an alliance with the sun.
Together, they are a dynamic team.
And as the duo blazes life's trails,
Opportunities begin to be unveiled,
Exposing what was previously unseen.

A new day is born!
Yesterday is spent; it is gone.
Today is a courtesy at life's discretion
For tomorrow is never a guarantee.
The present is life's only certainty,
Another chance to make an impression.

Morning has broken!
Unlocked, the doors of life are open.
The pathway to growth lies before me.
Then spoke that voice from deep inside,
"The power of choice is yours; you decide.
This moment is your greatest opportunity."

A new day has begun!
With it, fresh challenges to confront.
The integrity of the human is on the line.
At times, it takes a daring leap of faith.
That one small step that opens the gate.
The journey begins with the spirit of the mind.

The privilege of a new day!
All of life in an explosive display.
The abundance of life to enjoy, embrace.
It swings as if like an open door.
The fulness of life is yours to explore.
Then, like the wind, gone without a trace.

All of Me

All of me loves all of me.
All of me in its entirety, all.
That all of me loves all of me.
All of me stands proud and tall.
All of me believes in all of me.
All of me, down to the very core,
That all of me believes in all of me.
All of me started believing more.
All of me supports all of me.
All of me! None of me stands alone.
That all of me supports all of me.
All of me sits as a cornerstone.
All of me encourages all of me.
All of me gives all of me its best.
That all of me encourages all of me.
All of me settles for nothing less.
All of me has faith in all of me.
All of me was once walking blind.
That all of me has faith in all of me.
All of me is now renewed in mind.
All of me challenges all of me.
All of me makes all of me better.
That all of me challenges all of me.
All of me works as a team, together.
All of me empowers all of me.
All of me helps all of me improve.
That all of me empowers all of me.
All of me is a winning attitude.
All of me listens to all of me.
All of me—even the still, small voice—

That all of me listens to all of me.
All of me can rise above the noise.
All of me promotes all of me.
All of me furthers my every cause.
That all of me promotes all of me.
All of me looks beyond the flaws.
All of me celebrates all of me.
All of me honors the whole of life.
That all of me celebrates all of me.
All of me salutes the winner inside.
All of me respects all of me.
All of me is a role model.
That all of me respects all of me.
All of me leads by example.
All of me embraces all of me.
All of me takes all of me as I am.
That all of me embraces all of me.
All of me stands as a stable man.
All of me inspires all of me.
All of me helps all of me to grow.
That all of me inspires all of me.
All of me is now equipped to sow.
All of me nurtures all of me.
All of me feeds all of me its fill.
That all of me nurtures all of me.
All of me has an empowered will.
All of me loves all of me,
All of me completely, the whole.
That all of me loves all of me.
All of me is encouraged, in control.

Band of Brothers

That bond between blood brothers!
Indescribable—it is second to no other.
And though ours is of a different strain,
It is structured just the same.
Similarly, too, we share a unique bond.
We are a team, one for all and all for one.

Ours is founded on a certain discipline.
That code, the guiding principle within,
A common understanding of who we are.
Service above self, that which we stand for.
Above and beyond, we push on through.
Driven by passion, we just love what we do.

Our strength is grounded in togetherness;
A united approach ensures greater success.
Individually, each one is a pillar of support,
And together, we bolster, protect, promote.
We are a team; we are each one for the other.
The power of community, a band of brothers!

One mind, one goal boosts core confidence.
We trust each other's abilities and strengths.
Whatever the challenge we have to confront,
Banded together, we advance as a team of one,
Committed to the cause, wherever it may lead,
Bonded by code, we are driven to succeed.

This bond is built on a foundation of trust.
Primary, above all else, the cornerstone of us.
Without it, this exercise would be all but lost.
The ultimate sacrifice must be worth its cost.
Our base is strengthened by working together.
The spirit of community, a band of brothers!

This—what we do—is not for the faint of heart.
None but a selfless spirit can travel this path
To embrace service above self as an opportunity,
A willingness to deny self before honor, humility.
Bonded, each one a pillar of support for the other,
We are a special breed! We are a band of brothers!

Be Yourself

Be yourself!
There is no profit in being anyone else.
Develop your own set of standards.
Lay your own foundation to stand on.
You were created special and unique.
As such, there is no reason to compete.
You are worth as much as everyone else,
And even more valuable being yourself.

Be you!
To yourself endeavor always to be true.
Dare to be different; set yourself apart.
Walk in the integrity of your own heart.
Assert your uniqueness of individuality.
Establish and culture your own identity.
Embrace that sense of purpose and value.
Let it be worth your while to just be you.

Be strong!
Find your center, that place you belong.
Make a firm decision to live your best life
Despite it all; seize that moment to smile.
You will encounter challenges and trials.
Do not be fooled or blinded by denials.
You are not yet beaten; stand your ground.
There is greater deep within you, Overcome!

Be lowly!
Life does not revolve around you solely.
Be mindful before honor comes humility.
Be empathetic; have a heart for humanity.
None of us can independently stand.
At times, even the strong needs a helping hand.
Only a fool in his folly is convinced he knows it all.
A word to the ill-advised: Pride goes before a fall!

Be happy!
Praise and celebrate every personal victory.
Live the fullness of life; don't just simply exist.
Seize the moment; live your life to its fullest.
Empower yourself; put your whole you into it.
Be bold in your defiance of the accepted limits.
Be daring and dashing; step out and explore.
Live without borders; life is a wide-open door.

Be thankful!
Consider the gift of life; it is good and wonderful,
Regardless of whatever life may throw your way.
If only for the breath, be thankful for a new day.
No two days are alike; neither are any the same.
Notwithstanding, we are each an agent of change,
Each gifted with the power of choice in hand.
Be your best at being you, such as only you can.

Blessed Assurance

"Blessed Assurance," that amazing song of promise!
Nothing else in life is more reassuring than this.
A divine affirmation, a magnificent delight.
Even the very thought of the promise excites.
Fearfully and wonderfully made, perfect and entire.
All of life in abundance, according as desired.
And notwithstanding the near tragic fall from grace,
The expression of love secured the promise in its place,
A consideration none can fathom or even understand.
But faithful, according to promise, an unbreakable bond
Created in the image and likeness of a supernatural will
To honor and glorify, while enjoying the bounty, his fill.
The fullness of life, all at our disposal and pleasure.
An abundance of favors ever unfolding beyond measure,
Each one uniquely gifted and within each, his mustard seed.
The richness of life, according to whatever his need.
All of life in the palms of his hands, favored with abundance.
The only ask, obedience and an adherence to instructions.
The pride of creation! Highly favored over all the earth.
Blessed with a proven assurance beyond such as it deserves.
The free will of choice at its discretion, the power of control
Richly blessed, highly favored, with an abundance untold.
But emotions blinded reason, and the heart got in the way.
It became as if a stumbling stone, and he fell like an easy prey.
His eyes then became wide open; he confronted the naked truth.
The weed of lies trounced the seed of life, and he ate forbidden fruit.
Shamed and disenfranchised, his was a terrible fall from grace.
The pride of all of creation had fallen by the error of his ways.
It was the birth of a new beginning; his future was unknown.
An exile from his privileged place, far from his comfort zone.

15

For the first time in his existence, survival came by his hands.

The loss of his elevated sense of place heralded the fall of man.

As challenges and trials mounted, he was easily overwhelmed.

Falling out of favor with life, his was a seemingly a bitter end.

And at the break of each new dawn, the light exposed the truth.

Following his tragic fall from grace, he was lacking, fell destitute.

With each new day, the obvious; he was fast losing control.

With no viable hope of redemption, emptiness was taking its toll.

Losing his sense of balance, he was standing on unstable ground,

And with his mind deeply corrupted, he was easily brought down.

Still, he was not totally deserted; the heavens kept a watchful eye.

Man was never created to be a standalone; favor was standing by.

Moved by deep compassion, love emotionally reached out to man.

Manifesting the ultimate sacrifice, it became the sacrificial lamb.

The evils which had felled him, more cunning than he could tell.

Without a divine intervention, man could not have saved himself.

Yet man maintains the error of his ways, and day by day, the more,

While the promise which secured his victory remains intact, sure.

One moment the pride of creation, then, a lost and troubled soul.

But the promise which embraced him expresses a love untold.

The evils which corrupted him also disturbed his sense of place.

But the promise which embraced him is a gift of an amazing grace,

Favor which tells of a never-ending love, though undeserved, yet is.

"Blessed Assurance," that inspirational song of certainty and promise!

Breaking Out

I am a ferocious, angry, raging beast!
Caged, I am trapped deep within myself.
Blind fury is my chosen avenue of release.
I am a caged predator, but it is all in my head.
It is deep rooted and seated at the very core.
Breaking out is beginning to take a toll on me.
Considering the ever-growing bursts of uproars—
Unprovoked—control is slipping away gradually.

I growl in fierce anger even at the passing wind.
It has become a very vexing and irritating threat.
I become violently enraged at the simplest things,
Anything which finds its way past my safety net.
There is a red line surrounding my personal space.
I have become as a wild animal in a cage.
Any forced attempts at entry are treated with haste,
Such is met with bursts of aggression and rage.

Like a feared predator on the thrill of the hunt,
As if I am stalking a weak and unsuspecting prey,
The attack, executed with precision, is blunt,
And no consideration for whomever is in the way.
I am on constant alert for any intruding force,
Any measure of activity detected along my paths.
A failure to detour from this ill-advised course
Results in the unleashing of an intense wrath.

Each day proves daunting in the exercise of control.
Each new day is proving an impossible battle to win.
The exercise has already realized quite an exacting toll.
Day by day, breaking out is securing its place within.
Daily I battle in unrelenting earnest to recover myself.
Breaking out has caused me to shoulder needless loss.
So, too, the hideous voices echoing deep in my head.
With each passing day, I grapple with mounting costs.

And as I battle this menace, this embedded force,
Each day it gradually lays claim to valuable ground.
I stand virtually helpless, defenseless, and exposed.
Trying to reverse this curse is slowly weighing me down.
Daily the battle continues, though seemingly in vain.
Mine is a desperate search for any avenues of escape.
Breaking away also brings with it its own cache of pains.
But breaking out is slowly laying waste to my mental state.

Chasing a Dream

If only you were still a man!
Only then you might understand.
But now I am like a voice in the wind,
A mere speck of an inconspicuous thing,
Standing in the shadows of what you have become,
Quietly observing, as if taking refuge from the sun.
You have risen to an image of iconic stature.
The man you once were exists no longer,
Showered and adorned with glowing accolades.
Gone are those shadowy and invisible days.
In those days, it was only you and me.
I was the only one in the world you did see.
We shared a very connected and spirited bond.
It was the safest place being touched by your hands.
My heart still remembers each promise you made.
I felt so protected being held in your embrace.
There was an uplifting pride in our bonded duo.
I was your little champion, and you were my hero.
But lately you found membership on a different team.
Since then, I am left in the dust, trying to chase a dream
As the world lavishly celebrates your successes with you.
The distance keeps growing wider between us two.
Being caught up in your celebratory winds of change,
Transformed into a figure of prominence and fame,
Bonded by a mounting schedule of demands each day,
The image of your face is quietly fading away.
If only you could somehow see the many tears!
Or my voice was not so soft that you might hear!
These people would never be able to understand
I am forced to adjust to the touch of strangers' hands.

This is a cruel and evil world; it is not the same.
Their words of comfort are simply spoken in vain.
As my life dwindles day by day, I simply exist.
I stare idly at the distance, as if into the abyss,
Denying to myself those days have come to an end.
I anxiously await the return of my hero and friend.
Such as what this life has turned out to be!
I curse life for this very evil it has done to me.
But as you and your new circle celebrate and rejoice,
Remember the fading echoes of this juvenile voice.
My heart is learning daily to live without you.
The world has found its place in between us two.
As the distance grows wider, so are you in my sight.
Perhaps someday I may be awakened by a familiar light.

Cherish

Life, that mist, that gust of wind!
As brief as the air that is breathed in.
Like the light touting the breaking of dawn.
An inhale and exhale, and then it is gone.
Strung by the rhythms of a beating heart,
The music ceases when the beat is cut short.
Along this journey of one thousand miles,
At each turn, the ever-changing scenes of life.
From sunrise to sunset, at intervals in between,
The brevity and the fullness of life in every scene.
Each scene tells a story, every story plays its role
In the grand scheme of things as the journey unfolds.
In life's natural progression, each scene will change.
Like each day is dynamic, so no two are the same.
There will be some which are beyond the scope of man,
And then those a direct result of the works of his hands.
There will be some so impacting they will last a lifetime.
Some that will provoke the heart and engage the mind.
But each, notwithstanding, fits into a particular space.
Each with a specific purpose and in its rightful place.
Some scenes will upset balance; it won't be easy to stand.
There will be many which will test the resolve of man.
At times there will be questions when life overwhelms.
Insane searches for answers to help make sense.
And as emotion blinds reason, in a state of confusion,
It may seem convenient to blame life for the intrusion.
But with each new day, as the journey continues on,
Like daylight accompanying the breaking of dawn,
We will rise with the light when greeted by the sun
And open up to the new day which has just begun.

We will do so with little effort, as instinct dictates,
Forward in momentum, notwithstanding the aches.
As time goes by, we will heal as we continue to grow.
We will continue our journey and adjust as we go.
On occasions, we will stop and look back at the distance
To recall special moments which defined our existence.
And at some points along the way, life will reach into us
And humble the heart with thoughts as it rebuilds trust.
We will stop momentarily and withdraw to ourselves,
And relive specific moments, all alone, with no one else.
The memories will provoke as we quietly reminisce,
And held with a certain value, we will honor, cherish.
In that one brief encounter, we will then come to realize
That we were looking at life through the wrong set of eyes.
And as the mind becomes engaged by this new reality,
We hold a greater sense of appreciation for our own frailty.
And as we become more mindful of the uncertainties of life,
The mind becomes more open as we see through its eyes.
And as we consider all the things taken for granted each day,
We acknowledge the brevity of life, that it stands in the way.
Yet the fullness of life, unfolding, continues to keep giving,
To be enjoyed, unrestrained, by those who are truly living.
The various challenges and trials we every so often confront.
Though beyond comprehension, they influence the outcome.
In the natural order of things, as the journey of life unfolds,
Every scene that is played has its purpose and role.
The favors of life may not grant our every desire and wish,
But the abundance of its favors is to be honored, cherished.

Colors of Love

My life has never been this green!
Fertile. Fruitful. A refreshing scene!
It tells of blossoming fields of hope,
A vibrant harvest of explosive growth.
It signals an overwhelming abundance.
The seeds were plentiful in substance.
Abounding; it is more than enough.
Green is the color of love!

My life has never been this white!
Radiating. Glittering. A ray of light!
The darkness was as a crimson stain,
Deeply scarred, a dark, ghastly reign.
But then a brilliance, a life shone anew.
A beam of light came piercing through.
Glowing. A radiant glare from above.
White is the color of love!

My life has never been this red!
Ignited. Vehement. Forging ahead!
Passions inflamed; the heart is on fire.
Fueled by purpose, will burn higher.
Irrespective of the challenges of the day,
The ultimate goal is a heartbeat away.
Undaunted. An intense, heated rush.
Red is the color of love!

My life has never been this golden!
Favorable. Promising. Life wide open!
Precious and enriching, a glitzy bloom.
Optimism driven by a favor of fortunes.
A thriving abundance, a steady overflow,
An intense radiance as its favors grow.
Gleaming. Such as never dreamed of.
Golden, the wonder of love!

My life has never been this colorful!
Striking. Bold. Some kind of wonderful!
A flowering magnificence in vivid array.
Splendor and variety on grand display.
A kaleidoscope of colors bursts forth.
Life erupts into an explosion of growth.
Contented. The heart looks up above.
Colorful is the favor of love!

Compromise

The road of life is a complexity of confrontations.
Oftentimes, they unfavorably impact communication.
And every so often, instead of an act of compromise—
The channel through which a solution usually lies—
And with escalating emotions leading to a breakdown,
In the end, a lack of consideration for a middle ground.

A relationship was built over a lifetime of trust.
Years of mutual investment and sacrifice left to rust.
Even best friends often hold opposing views,
Differences of opinions over the most common issues.
And though in many a case dialogue will suffice,
The relations needlessly suffer for lack of compromise.

More often than not, when confronted by a stalemate,
With both sides suffering losses and huge costs at stake,
If but for consideration for the resulting damage and hurt,
An exercise in compromise could be a welcoming resort.
It by no means suggests a measure of weakness in any way.
But instead, a win-win solution designed to save the day.

Undoubtedly, to err is human, and to forgive is divine.
And every one of us loses our sense of place sometimes.
And because no one is perfect nor can any stand alone,
Others will have opinions different from our own,
And the sooner we humble ourselves and relax our pride,
The sooner we learn the valuable lesson of compromise.

Compromise has its place in the natural order of things.
When emotion blinds reason, it is the light which comes in.
So, too, when foolish pride threatens to dampen the day.
Compromise is the silver lining that clears the clouds away
It is not indicative of weakness; nor does it favor any side.
Instead, a sense of balance is reassured with compromise.

Compromise is the middle ground between conflicting sides.
It resets normal relations which would have otherwise died.
Compromise demonstrates character; it also promotes trust.
It encourages inner growth and helps the inner person adjust.
Compromise is surely an invaluable asset by any measure.
It is worth its weight in gold, certainly a priceless treasure.

Conflict

The continuous exercise of adjustments and changes!
The ever-changing scenes of life and its shifting stages.
The never-ending challenge to maintain a balancing act.
Life, constant in advance, powerless to hold itself back.
As evident with each new day, as life continues to unfold,
That constant battle of wills is an endless quest for control.
Highly favored by creation, his was a most privileged place.
But losing his sense of balance, he suffered a fall from grace.
There was no hidden agenda; man was perfect by creation.
Yet he caused his own discomfort by his desired inclination.
The evils which landed are ever intent on securing their fill.
Those external influences ever taunting the human will.
It was a case of misdirection, one small step by humankind.
He stained his own perfection by going beyond the line,
And with each passing day, as his many challenges grow,
Even the very gift of life seems his most formidable foe.
His is a never-ending struggle to maintain a sense of balance.
The evils up against him are unrelenting in their advance.
That which broke his mind had a hidden, sinister will.
Man, created perfect and entire, had become a broken spill.
The pride of creation, highly favored, richly blessed!
A conflict of interests has disrupted his completeness.
Ever prone to suggestion, he ceded his victory by deceit.
Notwithstanding, he has a willing spirit, but his flesh is weak.
The evils of the day prove more than cunning by design.
They know that the gateway to man's heart is fixed in his mind.
Lacking the discipline to adhere to an already charted course,
Daily, his is an endless battle to secure what he values most.
Considering his conflict of wills, a collision course with himself,
His very state of indecision presents a conflict within itself.

A very necessary evil, though occupying an unpopular space,
Conflict in life seems essential; it has its purpose and place.
The foundation of life is decision, though gifted by creation.
It has a greater purpose and meaning beyond any imagination.
Being conflicted with conflicts is the very essence of man.
Without which, man will lose himself in the very place he stands.

Dare

World, take notice, beware!
In time, you will learn I don't easily scare.
Even so, feel free to try as you may.
I openly welcome your challenge any day.
Go ahead, and give it your best shot.
Lay it all on me without holding back.
I know that you possess great power and might,
But I am standing my ground, poised for a fight.

Go ahead, world, make my day!
Do you have what it takes to blow me away?
It is widely rumored that you have great influence,
But is it enough to shatter my confidence?
Indeed, I have seen the things that you can do.
Notwithstanding, I am not intimidated by you.
I am aware of the number you have brought down,
The many hopes and dreams you buried in the ground.

World, I dare you, step up to the plate!
As powerful as you are, do you have what it takes?
But you do not just have to take me at my word.
Are you this mighty power of which I have heard?
How much I am anticipating that you will try!
Do not allow this grand opportunity to pass you by.
Oh, powerful and mighty world, I dare you, step out!
I want to experience for myself what you are all about.

Allegedly, you have destroyed many lives!
You are the reported cause of many a man's demise.
But as I study you intently each passing day,
I observe the types of minds on which you frequently prey.
Interestingly, the primary thing which amuses me the most,
The power you have amassed is not an impenetrable force.
As such, I have developed a good understanding of the game.
Those you managed to topple only have themselves to blame.

World, be warned, you cannot defeat us all!
And it will take more than you to cause me to fall.
Nevertheless, I am inviting you to give it a try.
This is a grand opportunity; do not allow it to pass you by.
I am waiting on you, world; consider my daring dare.
Rally your cache of resources; this is a personal affair.
Many have rumored that you are the big man on the block.
So world, I dare you to come at me without holding back.

Drug of Choice

I get extremely high on life!
My drug of choice, I need it to survive.
I consume as much of it as I can each day.
Whatever the cost, I am willing to pay.
I suffer from long-term use, an addiction.
It is past recreational; there's a deep conviction.
Without it in my system, I have no voice.
Nothing compares with it; it is my drug of choice.
Such as I have done with it, words cannot describe.
It is difficult to express how I am feeling inside.
It opens my mind, the way I think of myself,
I get so lifted, as if I am soaring above everyone else.
Whenever there is a challenge that I have to confront,
It gives an extra boost of power to help me overcome.
I treat it with respect because of its ability and strength.
A controlled, measured dosage ensures greater enjoyment.
To consume it in any other form but its natural state
Results in it being absorbed at a much faster rate.
The lower the quality, a higher likelihood of infection.
Exposed to constant abuse, the body sounds its objection.
I have seen many who suffered because of crash and burn.
Many were the warning signs, yet they waited too late to turn.
Some, through painstaking therapy, have remarkably survived.
Others fought to the finish, but sadly paid the ultimate price.
As with all drugs, it must be handled with a great sense of care.
Such a failure spells disaster; the consequences could be severe.
Still, despite of the long-term use, the addiction on the whole,
I am careful not to overindulge at the risk of losing control.
Failing to exercise caution, I could fall for lack of balance.
The drug is present everywhere; it is in great abundance.

It is extremely affordable and available on demand.
It is readily accessible, within easy reach of anyone.
I can use it at will with no fear of breaking any laws
If I don't deprive another without a probable cause.
Every drug has risk factors, new and developing concerns,
So I follow a rigid discipline before I, too, crash and burn.
To ensure a healthy status, I get tested from time to time.
Regular, periodic checks lead to a healthier state of mind.
I recommend its use to others in promotion of its benefits,
Providing them with factual data in my strong support for it.
Science has examined its structure—it was thoroughly analyzed—
It concluded that once used as directed, it leads to a healthier life.
The only side effect found promotes sheer folly and ignorance,
A failure to appreciate the dangers of abusing any substance.
As a result of long-term use, I need more and more each day.
Becoming an integral part of me, it is embedded in my DNA.
So once there is a breath in me, I will proudly sound my voice.
Above all that I have experienced, life is my drug of choice.

Emotion

Those unspoken words,
How deeply they hurt.
The silent language,
Consider the damage.
And tempers, once flared,
Take cover; beware
The things they can lead to!
Emotion can bleed you.

A strategic withdrawal,
The discretion to stand tall,
That familiar attitude,
An impending feud.
Often, when rumors spread,
Many become misled.
An explosive confrontation,
Little time for communication.

Some malicious, disruptive news,
Much debate on the issues,
Differences of opinions,
Open-forum discussions,
Presumed innocence attacked.
The truth becomes sidetracked.
Amid the confusion and rage,
Emotion takes center stage.

A once trusting heart, broken.
A reluctance to reopen.
A chance for healing and repair.
An emotional affair.
Words are kept at bay.
Obstacles stand in the way.
The heart is hardened inside.
Enter, foolish pride!

A natural, inescapable thing,
Emotion resides deep within.
Once it gets out of control,
The resulting damage is untold.
Still, it is a necessary evil.
Built in, it is unavoidable.
The things they often lead to!
Emotion only bleeds you.

Evergreen

If only time could recess here!
It is as fitting a place as anywhere else,
As life briefly pauses for healing and repair,
Deep down inside, I find peace with myself.
It is unlike anything this heart has ever seen.
Such stimulating magnificence to behold!
Amid the vast expanse of evergreen,
A renewing of the mind quietly unfolds.

A picture of disruptive beauty!
There is an uninhibited surrender within,
As if the still, small voice is speaking to me.
As a moth to flames, so am I to the wind.
All alone, engaged by whispering silence,
A refreshing newness lights across my face.
The peace and stillness, warmth of ambience,
I am lifted; my cares are gone without a trace.

Exciting the senses as it comforts, soothes,
It penetrates with a soft, therapeutic touch.
The air lazily strolls by with a quieting cool.
The spirit of the mind becomes awe struck.
As life is quieted and relaxes its hurried pace,
It openly welcomes the new fragrances in.
There is a total cleansing of its toxic wastes.
A quiet restoration takes place deep within.

It is truly a soulful and lifting moment!
Soul-searching! Awe-inspiring! Serene!
Reaching into me, it forces me wide open.
The heart submits to the power of the scene.
Running atop the distant, low, rolling hills,
Across the expansive, richly blanketed plains,
The engaging evergreen pierces with free will
Peace, such that even the heart cannot contain.

Peace of mind! Newness! Deliverance!
Life has enjoyed its total fill of inner peace.
The heart inhales, exhales in humble reverence.
The renewing of the inner person brings relief.
It tells of a welcoming and uplifting simulation.
The transformative powers of the evergreen!
Life is undoubtedly a miracle of transformation,
Unfolding and evident in its ever-changing scenes.

Exceptional

I am the exception!
There is nothing traditional about me—
A different path, another direction.
I am exceptional exceptionally!
Many prefer the paths of least resistance,
Their comfort zones; they feel safe, secure,
Unwilling to dare the uncharted distance,
Not willing to change the course, explore.
But I am the exception!

I am the exception!
Traditional will never characterize me,
My pathway to growth, progression.
I am exceptional exceptionally!
Many have avoided the roads less traveled.
Such roads tend to lead to parts unknown.
Corrupted in the mind, enslaved, shackled,
They lack the will to attempt the trek alone.
But I am the exception!

I am the exception!
Traditional: it will never become me!
A mind of my own, vital, essential.
I am exceptional exceptionally!
The mind is truly a terrible thing to waste.
Even so, many seem to lack a will to fight.
Broken in spirit, a clouded sense of place,
Darkness seems to block the guiding light.
But I am the exception!

I am the exception!
Traditional will not be embraced by me.
Driven and daring, informed, persistent.
I am exceptional exceptionally!
Nothing is as impossible as at times seems.
Where there is a will, there is always a way.
Anything is possible as long as one believes.
Nevertheless, fear has caused many to stray.
But I am the exception!

I am the exception!
Traditional proved too limiting for me.
Rising above to another dimension.
I am exceptional exceptionally!
Many have embraced the accepted limits.
No thought of or inclination to test the line.
Whether a fear of failure or broken spirit,
They starve all growth by staying behind.
But I am the exception!

I am the exception!
Traditional provides no comfort for me.
Growth-oriented, engaging potential.
I am exceptional exceptionally!
Adapted, the only thing to fear is fear itself.
So too, nothing ventured is nothing gained.
That one's greatest fear is a fear of oneself.
Yet to many, a retreat eliminates the pains.
But I am the exception!

Far and Away

Far and away …
Soaring to where the winds are at play.
Far and away from the cares of this world.
All alone, spirited and free, undisturbed,
Having no sense of urgency or duty of care.
Just me, all by myself, a solo, personal affair.
Far and away if but only for a brief moment.
A chance to repair all that has been broken.
Far and away …

Far and away …
Deep in the forests, where nature is at play,
Engaged by the embrace of the evergreens.
Life in full bloom, exploding in every scene,
Savoring the thrill of victory with each breath,
Watching defeat in its agony die a slow death.
Life being serenaded by the music of the wild.
A refreshing, lifting sensation brewing inside.
Far and away …

Far and away
As the dark of night is from the light of day,
To where the winds take whispered thoughts,
That place where secrets are buried in a heart.
Far and away, out of reach of the hands of time,
Beyond reach of the imaginations of the mind.
Far, far, and away, as the east is from the west,
To that place where a soul enjoys its fill of rest.
Far and away …

Far and away …
Beyond the horizon, at the edge of the day,
Across the oceans, the expanses of the seas
To unknown destinations as a passing breeze.
Far and away to humankind's earliest existence,
Like the echoes fading away into the distance
To the outer regions, the extreme of extremes.
Far away to places heard of yet never seen.
Far and away …

Far and away …
Above and beyond, where the angels play,
Deep in the heavens on the wings of a prayer.
Like that thought released into the atmosphere
Far, far and away, far above the circle of the sun.
Basking in the cosmos, the celestial playground,
Deep into the galaxy of stars, in a state of deity.
A chance encounter to escape this state of frailty.
Far and away.

Fear

It causes panic and despair!
A great misconception that surrounds fear,
Blamed for many a man's downfall
For obediently responding to his frantic calls.
Yet, like success which basks in its glory,
So too does fear tells its own story.
Portrayed as a cruel and menacing foe,
But fear in fact encourages courage to grow.

Interestingly, man is not alone!
It turns out that fear has fears of its own.
As I silently marvel over this irony,
Within, I am also amused at the calamity.
Though beaten, battered, and trampled under feet,
Yet does fear neither surrenders nor retreats.
While some consider fear as an evil demotivator,
Fear is no monster; instead, it is an innovator.

The embodiment of evil, demonized!
But fear is more a great blessing in disguise.
When left to itself, it is a mere powerless thing.
Fear only comes to life after it has been invited in.
If success is described as failure turned inside out,
Then fear is the element which challenges doubt.
Fear leads the charge to the renewing of the mind.
Fear challenges the inner man to go beyond the line.

Even a mysterious source of inspiration!
Many have been empowered by its stimulation.
It commands a deep, hidden, and powerful force.
The more it is engaged, the bolder courage grows.
Many a man have realized some incredible feats,
Acts which he is unlikely to ever consider a repeat.
But at the very moment he thinks of nothing else,
The only thing to fear is nothing but fear itself!

In fact, fear possesses fears of its own!
It cannot thrive in isolation, it fears being alone.
If only to make a mockery of the spirit of the mind,
Fear dares the inner man to brave the dividing line.
Fear's greatest of all fears is that of the human will.
Courage is the voice which causes fear to stand still.
If left all to itself then it will be all but laid to waste.
Fear relies on man for its identity and sense of place.

Food for Thought

Consider the majesty and glory of the lilies!
A blanket of radiance, clothing the naked fields.
Then an arid landscape, an abandoned waste
Transformed, life in living color, majesty ablaze.
The atmosphere is stirred with a lifting fragrance.
A splendor of magnificence, a scented radiance.
The ambience stimulates the senses deep inside.
A moving sensation experienced only by new life.

The explosive growth attracts a wealth of attention.
The return of life tells of a rebirth, a resurrection.
Then, outwardly lifeless, a bleak and empty scorn;
That which was seemingly dead has been reborn!
The arrival is heralded by vibrant, colorful cheers.
There is an exhilarating aroma stimulating the air.
The spirit of cleansing is inhaled with each breath.
The expression represents life's most inspiring yet.

The excitement unearths an amazing revelation.
Life is an infinite marvel of rebirth, transformation.
For it, on the surface, isn't as absolute as often seems.
The depth of life's powers is active behind the scenes.
To the unlearned, the arid soil appears a lifeless thing.
But greater is that power life holds deep within.
The mystery of life transcends the inmost imagination.
Continuous and dynamic, life is a marvel of creation.

The foundation of life proclaims an infinite will.
It is birthed by creation, predetermined to fulfill.
The picture on the surface is only half the truth told.
Deep within, the place where the real power unfolds.
The lilies in their wisdom seek to express the truth.
They know that the pathway to life is through its roots.
To the world, such surface may seem a lifeless ground,
But bearing the seeds to life within, the lilies overcome.

The ground may appear an arid and desolate waste,
And the season of gain may seem gone without a trace.
Nonetheless, notice the lilies, how they toil and grow!
Aware that they are key to their own growth, they sow.
Though the obstacles they encounter at times overwhelm,
Nonetheless, undaunted, they rely on their inner strength.
Theirs, too, is a brief encounter, like humans, as does all of life.
Nevertheless, they live colorfully; no breath is ever denied.

Friends

Friends!
What can be said about them?
They are like that precious gift.
They give a life that extra lift.
They are an invaluable find.
Their value grows with time.
What can be said about them?
It is good to have friends!

Friends!
They are truly heaven sent.
They are like angels-in-waiting.
Some, at your point of breaking,
Are like a sea of support;
They keep your ship afloat.
They are indeed heaven sent.
It is a blessing to have friends.

Friends!
Try and remember when
The light went out, no power.
You faced your darkest hour.
Then suddenly, out of nowhere,
At that instant a light appeared.
A stranger became your friend.
Can you remember when?

Friends!
You lost your way, but then …
Above the confusion, the noise,
That soft and reassuring voice.
Misled, somehow you went astray.
Then you were guided the other way.
It could have led you to a tragic end.
Have you ever been lost, but then …?

Friends!
Who can say you were one to them?
You went but did not want to go.
Or planted a seed so another can grow.
Perhaps that less unfortunate in need,
You stopped and did a selfless deed.
Can anyone say you were one to them?
Have you ever been such a friend?

Friends!
Maybe you are one of them.
You are masked as an altered ego,
But in the shadows, an unsung hero.
Maybe, by that single innocent act,
You helped to bring a lost soul back.
Unknowingly, you could be one of them.
A life is enriched by just being a friend.

Fullness of Life

I am living the fullness of life!
I am lifted with each inhaled breath.
Fullness beyond measure, it sets me aside.
This very moment is my most fulfilling yet.
The bounty of its favors overwhelms me.
I am reminded of how richly blessed I am.
An abundance at my disposal, undeservedly.
Notwithstanding, all part of life's master plan.

I smile with the gentle breezes blowing by.
Engaging and disarming, they reach into me.
There is a warm embrace from the sunlit sky.
A sense of belonging quietly flows through me.
The spirited winds echo with chuckling cheers.
My mind is moved by an amazement of thoughts.
Life's still, small voice permeates the atmosphere.
A fill of contentment settles deep within my heart.

I suffer no lack, neither in want nor need.
Such as I desire at that very hour, it is met.
Being highly favored, each new day, an increase.
The fullness has reassured me of my safety net.
My feet are grounded; a firm foundation was laid.
Life's favor of balance directs each step as I walk.
My heart is at peace, neither troubled nor afraid.
Even a fullness of light brightens life's every path.

Notwithstanding the fullness which abounds,
The evils of the day pose a never-ending threat.
Intent on weakening my balance, my very ground,
Nonetheless, powerless to penetrate my safety net.
For the battles before me, neither of them is mine.
Life's still, small voice encourages, "Peace, be still!"
An ever-present help by promise and ever on time.
The fullness I enjoy is gifted by a supernatural will.

I am highly favored with the fullness of life!
And with each given day is more, an increase.
The very thought humbles me; my cares subside.
There are no spoken words but a fill of inner peace.
The enemy is as daunting as the evils of the day.
They are both intent on disrupting my normal still.
But being favored by life, the evils are kept at bay.
The fullness of life is reassured by a superior will.

He Was Moved

He was moved …
He was moved because I stayed.
The evils had felled me, torn, wounded, and bruised.
And as I lay there, I collected myself and then prayed.
I cried out aloud, though I was worn and broken.
My strength was all gone; I lay weak and afraid.
And as I opened my heart, so the heavens opened.
He was faithful according to the promise he made.
He was moved …

He was moved …
He was moved because of my faith.
The fiery tongue burned me; I was unjustly accused.
Notwithstanding the fact that I fell, I did not break.
The enemy which bound me, it left me for dead.
I was deserted and cast aside, so downtrodden.
But encouraged by the Word, I lifted up my head.
Being favored, I was neither forsaken nor forgotten.
He was moved …

He was moved …
He was moved because I obeyed.
The evils of the day intended to destroy the truth,
But the foundation of the Word was already laid.
It is cunning in deception and a master of the art.
To denounce the truth, it declared a colorful prize.
They tried to break my mind by upsetting my heart.
But then a whisper, "Obedience is better than sacrifice!"
He was moved …

He was moved …
He was moved because I called.
I was lost and misdirected, intimidated and confused.
Broken in the spirit of my mind, I suffered a great fall.
Lurking fears of failure had pushed me beyond the line.
With each new day, I faced an ever-mounting struggle.
But a whisper in the storm came at the opportune time.
It reminded me, "I am an ever-present help in trouble!"
He was moved …

He was moved …
He was moved because I prayed.
The enemy scarred me; I was wounded and bruised.
My heart was deeply troubled; I was timid and afraid.
But encouraged by the Word, I was able to rise above,
And in the piercing light, the plain truth was revealed.
He was moved because of promise, yet more, his love.
He is moved for he is that ever-present help in need.
He was moved …

Hope

Hope: it is the will of growth!
Conviction with devotion, it is faith in motion.
A structured discipline that is centered deep within.
Embedded, innate, it is the beginning of faith.
Hope: it is the seed of growth!
The fruit of aspiration bred from inspiration.
The harvest of a thought cultivated in the heart.
That lone grain of mustard seed, a flourishing yield.
Hope: it is the foundation of growth!
The measure of the man taking a decisive stand.
The essence of the man within, character building.
Significant, and above all else, hope believing in itself.
Hope: it encourages growth!
It is a culture of thought which stimulates the heart,
Engaging the spirit, the inner man daring the limits.
Hope is the power of will refusing to remain still.
Hope: it is necessary for growth!
Unless the mind first moves, nothing can be proved.
When that of the still, small voice silences the noise,
It bears its rightful fruits consistent with its roots.
Hope: it is the pillar of growth!
The discipline to sow, ever the willingness to grow,
To discourage a retreat even in the face of defeat,
To be celebratory in advance of the thrill of victory.
Hope: it is essential to growth!
A fundamental element in character development.
Ceasing that moment in time to reassure the mind.
With a sound mental state, hope is a prelude to faith.
Hope: it is the gateway to growth!
The mind, that open door, the confidence to explore.

The spirit renewed, the mind adopting a new attitude,
Seizing the day, the will to get out of one's own way.
Hope: it empowers growth!
A reflection of a certain pride when standing side by side.
A giant of a man, life within easy reach of his hands,
The conviction to believe, faith as a mustard seed.
Hope: it is the essence of growth!
Embracing the embedded fears, the boldness to dare.
It is courage under fire, fortitude, and endurance inspired.
Hope is essential to life, that certain spirit which never dies.
Hope: it is life's engine of growth!

I Am

If only you knew who I am.
I am more than just a man.
I am every expression of my heart,
A direct reflection of my thoughts,
That voice of victory or defeat.
I am the very words that I speak.

I am my strengths and weaknesses,
My failures and successes.
I am my dreams and aspirations—
Even the power of imagination—
Whatever my mind can conceive.
I am that as I earnestly believe.

I am purpose defined.
I am my moment in time.
I am that bold and courageous dare.
I am my own greatest fear.
I am the decision to seize the day.
I am that mountain in my way.

I am the free will of choice,
The ability to rise above the noise.
That beacon of hope, burning bright
I am a reflection of that light.
This attitude of mine, now grown,
The fruit of that which I had sown.

I am that powerful force of energy,
The potential buried deep in me.
I am my actions and reactions,
My faults, flaws, and imperfections.
I am that piercing ray of light
That gives me power for the fight.

I am the foundation of my growth
That on which I build my hope.
I am my whole outlook on life.
I am that willpower to survive.
See, I am more than you imagined.
I am more than just a man within.

I Told Life

I told life!
There were so many things that I had to say.
The weight was overwhelming my heart.
I told life!
The burden told on me with each new day.
My state of mind had begun falling apart.
I needed to find someone with a sense of care,
Someone whose character demonstrated integrity.
I needed someone who would give me a listening ear
Someone with an open heart, warmth, and affinity.
So I told life!

I told life!
The truth was proving too hard to contain.
My emotions were getting the better of me.
I told life
That I would breathe the breath of love again!
I never imagined this day would ever be.
I withdrew to myself, so I could digest it all in stride.
It came at a time when there were lingering doubts.
I thought there was no more place in this broken life,
But somehow it found a way in and brought me out.
So I told life!

I told life!
The thrill of victory, that seemingly lifting treat!
Yet my victory proved more a disturbing affair.
I told life
This victory, it feels more like the agony of defeat.
There are upsetting echoes of voices everywhere.
Mine had been a life plagued with disruptive lows.
It seemed like my moment in time would never come.
Many stood by my side throughout my period of woes.
Still, as if undeserved, my victory is upsetting to some.
So I told life!

I told life!
Each given day, I travel along life's busy streets.
And time and again, I question man's sense of care.
I told life
At every turn, there are faces marred by ghastly defeat.
But more often than not, it is as if they are never there.
These streets know all about life; nothing hides from them.
Like a God, they know even the whispered thoughts of man.
Each day they lead the way, so man can solve his problems.
But such roads are less traveled by those with helpful hands.
So I told life!

I told life!
Creation must have possessed a great love for man.
I consider the bounty of favors which he enjoys.
I told life!
Being entrusted with the power of control in his hands,
As well as the freedom of will and the free will of choice,
Though the last of creation yet favored and chosen above.
Whatever are his heart desires, such he is never denied.
Above all of creation, man is blessed with a special love.
Still, despite it all, his insatiable hunger is never satisfied.
So I told life!

In Retrospect

In retrospect,
A moment in time to quietly reflect.
Recalling the spent years,
Life's natural process of wear and tear.
Looking over my life,
I am simply humbled to be still alive.
Time has favored me.
I am highly favored by life, undeservedly.

In retrospect,
As my train of thought silently redirects,
Revisiting the earlier days,
The soul is stilled by deep honor in praise.
Life is in total control.
As the moving images unwittingly unfold,
Emotions take hold of me.
Life is playing the scenes it wants me to see.

In retrospect,
The things that I see as I quietly reflect!
Life as never seen before.
The mind breaks out with a rushing outpour
As each image is revealed,
Even those I thought were lost and concealed.
It is an emotional affair.
A reflective engagement, it heals and repairs.

In retrospect,
Certain of the scenes set me back to regret
Near ill-fated tragedies of the past.
Many led to needless suffering and emotional loss.
I am provoked by deep thoughts.
A moment of sadness briefly settles in my heart.
If only it were possible somehow!
If only I knew then what I have come to know now!

In retrospect,
Never again am I likely ever to forget
That life is an amazing gift,
And I must make the best of even the worst of it.
Though there are trials and challenges,
Life is a journey of choices and consequences.
But as long as there is still life yet,
I will live it unrestrained until the very last breath …
In retrospect.

Incarceration

These walls are decorated with history.
They tell about those who came before me.
These are society's walls of shame,
And now they bear my name.
Echoes of past voices can still be heard
Penetrating this dark and restrictive world.
My sense of balance tips over the borderline.
Ridicule and sarcasm play with the mind.

The images expose deep-rooted hurt and
Questions of life, its value and worth.
Tales of the lives which have been displaced,
Imprisoned in this sullen and desolate space.
The emotions run far and deep,
And nights are a nightmare of restless sleep.
As my sanity slides closer to the dividing line,
Insanity battles for control of the mind.

Like a daily cycle of rehearsed scenes,
Day after day, a constant set of routines.
Time and day seem only that which change.
All else around me remains the same.
Life snails along as if with a handicap.
Scenarios of events repeatedly play back.
Silent tears slowly roll down my face.
Reality is gradually settling in place.

I stare at freedom with a meaningless gaze,
A mental recall of the glory days.
The soft-spoken voices of my formative years,
Like cymbals, they echo like chimes in my ears.
By failing to adhere to reason and advice,
I am now forced to pay this exacting price.
For ignoring the many cries of the inner voice,
This is the fallout from my misguided choice.

Now that these walls are bearing my name,
My life will forever carry an indelible stain.
Though I may grow with the passage of time,
This is one scar that I will bear for life.
Much in contradiction to popular belief,
To forget isn't one of life's greater luxuries.
Whilst the free will of choice is for us to make,
The consequences of such are for life to dictate.

Into the Sun

Many thought this day would never come!
They thought we could never walk into the sun.
That the thrill of victory, gone without a trace,
The agony of defeat is fixed in its place.
But banded together like pillars of support,
A unity of purpose brought reassuring hope.
Behind the dark clouds came a blinding light.
As the sun rose, it revealed a beautiful sight.

Today marks our defining moment!
The door to freedom swings wide open.
A bold new beginning, a piercing light,
The sun exposes the most amazing sight.
Today we march triumphantly into the sun,
Marching to the beat of a different drum.
Today we welcome a new wind of change.
Today our voices echo in a loud refrain.

It is the birth of a daring new courage.
Hope finds strength to brave the challenge.
Fear, once embedded, has been overrun.
Victory has not only been claimed but won.
The start of a journey of one thousand miles.
A new direction, no longer running as if wild.
A joyful return to the place where we belong.
Today time has corrected history's wrongs.

For years we were forced to stand down.
For years they crudely silenced our tongues.
As a silenced voice can never communicate,
So a mind corrupted will eventually break.
But a foundation was laid by many long ago.
The seeds they planted have begun to grow.
No retreat or surrender, no turning back.
As courage breaks free, fear is under attack.

The silence breaks into a symphony of songs.
The voices march triumphantly into the sun,
United for a common goal, the right to be free.
Freedom sings in a harmonious voice of victory.
As the voices vibrate through the atmosphere,
It is a signal to the world to be on alert, beware.
Never will we stand by and remain silent again.
As we march into the sun. we are changing lanes.

Journey

At long last, the journey home!
This day has been long anticipated.
It seemed like forever we have waited,
But the seeds we have planted are grown.
The fruits of our labor which we have sown,
And the sacrifices made have not gone to waste
For today, our own sense of place!
Today we reclaim our right of identity.
Today we remind the world of our right to be.
Time has corrected history's wrongs.
The foundation we build on is solid, strong.
Today we reclaim what is rightfully our own.
Today we begin that long journey home!
From this day onward, our very own names.
Today we have broken that suppressive chain.
Until today, we were seemingly unknown,
But finally, our identities are our very own!
Memories of the heartland were never erased.
Today, a triumphant return to our rightful place!
This moment is more precious than that of gold.
Today we begin our long journey home!
Though our bodies bear wounds of upsetting scars,
And tears tell tales of a dreaded and horrid past,
And though we are all smudged with indelible stains,
Notwithstanding, the sacrifices were not in vain.
Indeed, the full could never be told!
But today we begin our long journey home.
And while scars would remain over the passage of time,
We have finally broken that which had broken our minds.
Today we express ourselves with the unity of voice.

The whole world will hear us as our hearts rejoice.
Our singing will echo across the vast expanse.
The whole earth will vibrate as we revel and dance.
There will be a thundering in the atmosphere.
As the silence is ruptured, the whole would will hear.
The agony of defeat may speak of our broken history,
But our songs of freedom will tell of the thrill of victory.
Though we once fell because we were broken in mind,
We encouraged ourselves; then fell the dividing lines.
This victory is for the generations to come.
They will enjoy their own places under the sun.
Yesterday may not have been our own,
But today, at long last, our journey home!

Life Is Choice

Life is a matter of choice!
It is an individual and powerful voice,
A divine gift given to man by creation.
He is the sole architect of his destination.
A favor of life enjoyed only by man,
He holds the power of choice in his hands.
Regardless of person, stature, or mental state,
He is the power which decides whatever his fate.
In life, man will be challenged on every given day.
There will always be mountains standing in his way.
Defeat or overcome, a decision he alone must make.
Death provides his only avenue of escape.
Choice is power, the independent will to stand.
A privilege and consideration gifted to man.
From the beginning, it was placed in man's hands.
He alone must decide where he chooses to stand.
Inevitable and certain, none of us can escape.
Man is a product of the choices he makes.
Free will to act but instead an omission,
And that in itself is an actual decision.
By stillness of the tongue the wise rejoice.
But that very act of silence is a passive choice.
The freedom to decide the choices he may make,
But the outcome which follows is not his to dictate.
The independence of will, absolute by design,
An ability to appreciate with a sound, balanced mind.
Uniquely gifted by creation, enjoyed solely by man,
None other holds the power of choice in hand.
Silence may be golden, but it is, in fact, a powerful voice.
Life, that gift of creation, is ultimately a matter of choice.

Life

Life, that marvel and gift of creation!
An amazement of wonder, pure admiration
Filled with a splendor too wonderful for words,
Speaks in a voice which only spirits have heard.
Contained within itself, like that of a seed,
An unfolding abundance, whatever the need.
A touch of sensation that humbles the soul.
Memories to treasure more precious than gold.
Each day is dynamic; no two are alike, the same.
A marvel even the heart cannot fully contain.
An explosion of beauty, provocative, serene,
A kaleidoscope of colors in every scene.
Life uninterrupted, no needless duty of care.
The mind is the limit; it is an attitude affair.
A wide-open door, nature's favor to man,
The power of choice in the palms of his hands.
A journey which begins at the very first breath,
comes to its end at the hour of death.
It will field challenges and trials along the way,
And obstacles will surface on every given day.
Courage may come under fire; even hope may fade.
There will be setbacks, even with the best plans laid.
Faith will be tested, and patience will grow thin.
A constancy at failing may silence the will to win.
Nonetheless, they do no injury to life's master plan
For the favors of life are still at the disposal of man.
To some, life may seem broken, futile in aspiration,
But it is not the gift that's flawed; it is the application.
Man's hunger for growth has taken an exacting toll.
The explosion of knowledge tells of his lack of control.

By being driven to succeed at whatever the cost,
Man's mind has become corrupted, and his balance is lost.
His is a world which is fractured, collapsing within itself.
Assuredly on a collision course, man up against himself.
And in the meantime, life continues at a constant pace,
Never once encouraged to compete in the human race.
But at the appointed hour, if man does come around,
Life in great abundance can still be easily found.
For life remains obedient to its purpose and will.
Such as man's heart desires, life obediently fulfills.
Life, that marvel and gift of creation,
It meets man at his needs; he is his own limitation.
An abundance of favors, all provided in advance,
The fullness of life within easy reach of his hands.
Over all of creation, in its entirety, the whole,
Man is so highly favored that he is granted control.
With the power of choice and the freedom of will,
Once he can imagine it, life is duty bound to fulfill.
The fullness of life—whatever his heart may desire—
An abundance of favors, accordingly as required.
Indeed, his is the freedom to decide the choices he makes,
Though the consequences which follow aren't his to dictate.
Even so, this wonder and marvel is creation's gift to man.
Life, in all its fullness, in accordance with the master plan.

Memory Lane

Those were the days!
Life has since changed in many ways.
I simply marvel at the years gone by.
I am amazed at the speed by which time flies.
And as I sit and quietly reflect,
Retracing life's journey from the earliest step
From the dawn of its beginning,
It is indeed an amazing thing!

Time has undeservingly favored me.
The many things it has allowed me to see.
Unmasking the years through a mental slideshow,
A timeline of events from the days of long ago.
Engaged by the silence of the moment,
Moved by deep thoughts, the mind is forced open.
And as the images quietly unfold,
Life at this stage assumes complete control.

It seemed like just yesterday,
Though life has since journeyed quite a long way.
Countless images have become vividly clear.
The many echoes of the past I am able to hear!
I stare idly as if into the abyss.
Life reduces its pace as I quietly reminisce.
It is a long, solitary walk down memory lane,
Temporarily reliving the spent years over again.

Privately, as I retrace the passage of time,
A stampede of events races across my mind.
It was quite an experience, this invasion of thoughts!
A flood of emotions gushes out of my heart.
The exercise had unwittingly lifted me off my feet.
The mind was in control of this mental retreat.
It turns out that nothing is ever truly forever lost.
Life maintains records of everything from its past.

As I quietly stroll down memory lane,
There are moments of laughter, sadness, and pain.
I struggle to conceal and maintain my composure.
All of life seemed relieved from the mental exposure.
Life—it is indeed such an amazing gift!
And I vow to make the best of even the worst of it.
Notwithstanding whatever life may throw my way,
I intend to live it to the fullest with each given day.

Mental Slavery

The mind is indeed a terrible thing to waste!
Even more so, the loss of a man's sense of place.
By simply evading his independent will to stand,
To assert his own identity, the measure of a man,
To open up to the influence of an imposing will.
A man who is broken in mind is a costly rebuild.
The enemy, ever watchful, is relentless by design,
With a never-ending quest to control of the mind.

Man is his own worst enemy, his greatest of all.
More often than not, he causes his own downfall.
Ever prone to suggestion, he leads himself astray.
Then caught in a snare, he becomes an easy prey.
The very thought is a scourge, a calamity,
That a mind would freely discard its individuality
By submitting to a standard that can never fulfill,
To surrender complete control by its own free will.

It is said the only thing to truly fear is fear itself.
Yet that miscarriage of thought often overwhelms.
For a man becomes that as he thinks in his heart,
An outward reflection of his deep, inner thoughts.
A mind follows that as it had been led to believe.
It bears fruits consistent with the cultured seeds.
Prone to suggestion, obedient to such as is sown,
The mind, like man, also has a mind of its own.

Man is the author and finisher of his own fate,
The freedom to decide on the choices he makes.
With the power of will in the palms of his hands,
The direction of his growth is determined by man.
Whilst the favors of life are gifted to all equally,
That each such measure was allotted favorably,
And knowing that the mind is his center, his fill,
Yet man submits to the voice of an imposing will.

Tragic, those who fall prey to mental slavery!
To surrender to the will of an invasive ideology.
The ones who have the seeds but refuse to sow,
Having the power of choice but unwilling to grow.
There are those who inadvertently were led astray;
In searching for an identity, they fell along the way.
The invading forces blocked their avenues of escape.
The imposition of wills disturbed their mental states.

The mind is certainly a terrible thing to waste!
Enslaved by suggestions is a dire fall from grace.
In the battle of wills, each holds a duty to himself.
He is his own primary responsibility above all else.
Having his own identity, he has a sovereign voice.
To be enslaved by suggestion is an individual choice.
The mind, a strategic and critical seat of command!
That which controls the mind also controls the man.

Mind, My Business

Charity begins at home.
The heart always feeds itself first.
That the duty of self-growth is my own,
I am ever mindful to avoid the obverse.
It has the disposition of a child
In constant need of attention and care,
Prone to influence, susceptible, fragile.
Unattended, it becomes a predator's lair.

The mind is a coveted prize.
It holds the seat of power for man
For in the mind is where man resides.
It is his base of control and command.
I must remain watchful, ever on alert.
Such a failure may lead to a tragic fall.
He who loses his mind is of little worth.
Whoever controls the mind controls it all.

The mind is the battleground.
A vast wealth of abundance it holds.
The ultimate prize, it is second to none,
It is worth more than its weight in gold.
A bounty of resources, unlimited in power,
A balanced sense of place, a venerable prize.
With limitless fields of potential to discover
That the threat is real can never be denied.

The enemy is a formidable foe.
It remains tactful as it craftily waits,
Maintaining its vigilance wherever I go.
At a given moment, I could seal my fate.
All of man resides within his mind,
And without it, he is of no value or worth.
Conscious that this is the fight for my life,
I must be ever conscious, on constant alert.

Evil wears many a face.
Many are wolves disguised as sheep.
It could be a genial smile or an embrace.
Or friendly advice encouraged by deceit.
The mind, my business, my responsibility.
It is mine to protect at whatever the cost.
Mindful what's at stake, I give it all of me.
The alternative could be a tumultuous loss.

Each day, new challenges lie ahead.
The enemy is relentless in its quest.
I must remain alert, so I won't be misled.
The enemy doesn't, so neither must I rest.
The evils of the day lie cunningly in wait,
Intent on breaking the spirit of my mind.
Any shift in focus, and I may seal my fate.
The mind, my business, my affair, full time.

Music Is Life

Music is the foundation of life!
From an unfathomable imagination
That gave birth to the marvel of creation,
The beginning strung the orchestra alive.
Out of the murky darkness, revealed
Light and life in an explosion of scenes.
Music laid the foundation for life.
As the voice commanded, "Let there be,"
Speaking with power and authority,
Music, for the first time, was realized.
As the master plan gradually unfolded,
Rhythmic and spirited, music exploded
Music is the foundation for life!

Music is the rhythm of life!
It jolts the thumps of the beating heart.
It fuels each breath to an active start.
That music powers us forward excites!
Emotion is a drum of one thousand beats.
It serenades a mind with melodious treats.
Man strings whatever chords he decides.
Personalized, it tells of an intimate affair.
Man plays the music that he prefers to hear.
He moves to whatever melodies seem right.
And though he plays it by ear sometimes,
He sets his own stage as he designs.
Music sets the rhythm for life!

Music is the song of life!
The soul of man is a living symphony.
It vibrates the senses with musical harmony.
The whole of man becomes awakened inside,
Be it the sound of a voice or a chuckling cheer,
An explosive laughter rippling through the air.
The atmosphere is abuzz with audio bites,
Whether the rustling winds or the roaring seas
Or the massaging touch of a therapeutic breeze.
The uplifting melodies of the music of the night!
Even in the penetrating and deafening still,
The silence breaks open with a melodious thrill.
Music is the song of life!

Music is the food of life!
Healthy and nutritious, its benefits are untold.
It is a highly recommended food for the soul.
It promotes a sound, well-balanced state of mind.
Rated by every standard as a natural supplement,
Potent, it is pure and very energy efficient.
It is an aphrodisiac which keeps the senses alive.
Abundant in supply, it can be found everywhere.
Its cost is inexpensive, and it can be easily prepared.
It is an extremely rich and tasty delight.
Consumed naturally, it is at its most nutritious yet.
Among its many qualities is its stimulating effect.
Music is the food of life!

Night Fever

The heat is on!
The temperature rises when the lights go off.
As the darkness asserts command and control,
The terrors of the night begin to unfold.
As the light retreats into another realm,
The creatures of the night assume the helm.
Having no restrictions, as the night rolls on,
They rule the darkness till the break of dawn.

The breeze, once a gentle touch in the dusky fill,
Now a haunting evil, an echo of an eerie chill.
Even cracks and crevices offer a welcome embrace,
A most unwelcome intrusion into personal space.
As the darkness deepens, the howling intensifies.
The heartbeats increase as the temperatures rise.
There is a feverish encounter in the darkened chill,
A hair-raising incursion as the terrors move at will.

Creepy, shadowy figures parade back and forth.
The darkness, their superior, renders full support.
Invasive masked avengers, theirs is the advantage.
An army of silhouettes with free will unchallenged
The foundation is unsettled, it is exposed to its core.
The mind becomes overpowered; its collapse is sure.
Haunting tales from a broken past tell of the fright.
The miseries of the deep have befriended the night.

Alone and exposed to the taunts of the dark sphere,
Screams are a choking whisper; enter, nightmares!
Paralyzed with deep fears of an impending doom,
There seems no avenue of escape from the eerie tomb.
As the darkness advances and the terrors parade,
As the mind lies exposed and the will to fight fades,
The melodies which once lifted the spirit inside
Are now a morbid intrusion, distorting the mind.

The heat is on!
And with miles to go before the return of dawn.
As the darkness lauds over its command and control,
The evils of the night have caused real damage untold.
At the return of dawn, with the new light of day,
If only the daylight could retain an extended stay!
That the darkness would disappear without a trace;
If only the darkness never again returns to this place!

No Limits

Dare the impossible!
Dream the improbable!
You are whatever your thoughts!
Set yourself apart!
Confront boldly that challenge!
Embrace it with courage!
A winner never quits!
Observe no limits!

Difficult, yet possible, believe!
As small as a mustard seed!
Take it one step at a time;
Begin with an end in mind!
Take control of the advantage!
Develop a thirst for knowledge!
Empower yourself; grow with it!
Observe no limits!

It is possible; it can be achieved!
Become one with your dreams!
Your gift is unique and special!
You own your greatest potential!
Elevate yourself with confidence!
Be daring; make a difference!
Power on the winner's spirit!
Observe no limits!

Before honor comes humility!
Have a heart for humanity!
Your character defines you;
To yourself always be true!
Wealth and fame may bring you much,
But never lose that common touch!
Be ever mindful of the days of old;
Their value is as precious as gold!

No two days are ever the same,
But you are an agent of change!
Greater is the power within you;
Just imagine what you can do!
Give it your all, your very best,
And in return, accept nothing less!
Remember, a winner never quits!
Winners observe no limits!

One Day in Time

One day in time—
As long as life favors me still–
I will be pouring my fill.
Abundance will be as predestined
One day in time.
As long as I maintain control.
Once I remain focused on the goal,
I will realize that dream of mine
One day in time.

One day in time,
The seeds have already been sown.
In time they will be fully grown.
A great harvest is next in line.
One day in time,
I will be favorably rewarded.
The process has already started.
As sure as the sun does shine
One day in time.

One day in time,
Having conquered the agony of defeat,
The thrill of victory now being my treat.
I have a new attitude developing inside.
One day in time,
As the darkness gradually disappears,
Since overcoming my deepest fears,
I will become a winner by design.
One day in time.

One day in time,
With the power of choice firmly in my hands
And working according to a master plan,
I am reasserting control over my life,
One day in time.
Aware of my weaknesses and strengths,
I am rebounding with confidence.
I will no longer be left behind
One day in time.

One day in time,
Celebration will come my way.
I can already see that wonderful day.
The image is fixed firmly in my mind.
One day in time,
Discovering more about who I really am,
I am becoming a giant of a man.
My mountains will be much easier to climb
One day in time.

One day in time,
As long as life favors me still,
I won't be resting until
I lay claim to that illustrious prize.
One day in time
I will be enjoying my just reward.
The years of hard work will pay off
For I am still highly favored by life
One day in time.

Open Letter

Dear Love,
I felt compelled to write this letter to you.
I am just amazed at what you were able to do.
In quiet reflection, I am humbled in thought.
A sense of great gratitude overwhelms my heart.
Had it not been for you, I'd have died long ago.
What you planted in me is beginning to grow.
By investing your time, potential was realized.
The seeds that you planted are teeming with life.
A thought came to me as I sat by myself,
If you had never reached me, I'd already be dead.
That place you found me, I was beaten and worn,
At the hour of my death, at the point of no return.
You rescued me, though I never cried out for help.
You saved me when I was unable to save myself.
Now today, I am a towering giant of a man!
As if all of life is within easy reach of my hands.
I simply marvel at the man I have since become.
I am especially delighted by what you have done.
You have created a new mind in me,
Transforming the old man into a new identity!
I am humbled and overwhelmed; I am deeply moved,
Excited, and delighted but still somewhat confused.
Your embrace has lifted me; I was all but corrupted.
If left all to myself, I would have soon self-destructed.
The world seemed to have shifted under me, and I fell.
Had it not, eventually I would have destroyed myself.
Not of my own doing; this rescue was not my design.
But death seemed not quite ready for me at the time.

Somewhere along the road of life, I lost my way.
I couldn't have found myself on the brightest day.
My mind was corrupted; I was deeply troubled within.
As much as I tried resisting, I had lost all will to win.
But at the appointed hour, a welcoming embrace
As if that which was missing was now suddenly in place.
There was like a new sense of purpose, as if a rebirth.
I thought, *Finally, I found life's meaning and worth!*
I felt lifted; there was a sense of heightened sensation,
As if on top of the world looking down on creation.
With each passing day, I was like a runaway train.
The power in me was more than I could contain.
Yet still, as much as I enjoyed, I grasped for more.
I had never experienced anything like this before.
A reckless endangerment, a menacing dare,
My sense of humanity had begun to disappear.
A power unto myself, having no need to control,
Too clouded to realize that it was taking its toll.
Then, unsuspectingly, a new day was dawning.
As if instantaneously, a new reality stormed in,
Defeated and overcome, my voice was silenced.
Powerless, still I stood in relentless defiance
Up against an invading force—by myself, alone.
There was no one within reach; I was on my own.
Emptiness infused, there was a deafening still.
That which corrupted me paraded with free will.
As never before, I was confused, afraid, and unsure.
I had never experienced fear quite like this before.
Then piercing the darkness, a light broke through.
I was temporarily blinded, and then there was you.
The moment you embraced me you eased my pain.
I was even more lifted when you called me by name.
The day that you found me, I had nowhere else to go.

That you came just to find me was all I needed to know.
Cheated and defeated, broken spirit, disturbed mind,
That moment you found me, you came just in time.
Beyond belief, unearthly! This amazing love of yours!
If only I could thank you! If only there were words!

Peace

Primary of my personal responsibilities, inner peace!
I could be standing face to face with a raging storm.
The enemy could intend me some physical harm.
But as long as I have my peace, I can find relief.
Fractures in my life could suddenly burst open.
The spirit of my mind could abruptly be broken.
But as long as I have my peace, I can find relief.
The evils of the day could pose a menacing threat.
Today could represent my most challenging yet.
But as long as I have my peace, I can find relief.
Friends could rise against me in any number of ways.
My circle could denounce me and deny me my place.
But as long as I have my peace, I can find relief.
Life could interrupt my normal state of good health.
Circumstances could disrupt my accumulated wealth.
But as long as I have my peace, I can find relief.
My voice could be silenced by a repressive regime.
My freedom could be threatened by tortuous means.
But as long as I have my peace, I can find relief.
Secrets could be revealed and promises made broken.
The pain of discomfort could leave my heart wide open.
But as long as I have my peace, I can find relief.
Confidence could be shaken by a sudden twist of fate.
Emotions could unsettle my otherwise normal state.
But as long as I have my peace, I can find relief.
Dark clouds could delay the silver lining behind.
The raging storms could linger for an extended time.
But as long as I have my peace, I can find relief.
My walk with kings could infect my common touch.
I could somehow lose myself in the company of such.

But as long as I have my peace, I can find relief.
Failure as an option could be absent from my mind
Yet the very thing I dread could just be the next in line.
But as long as I have my peace, I can find relief.
Weapons formed against me could for a while prosper.
Tragedy could strike even in an already active disaster.
But as long as I have my peace, I can find relief.
A case of misadventure could signal my fall from grace.
An ill-advised decision could disrupt my sense of place.
But as long as I have my peace, I can find relief.
My shoulders could be burdened with a sizable load.
The shirt I am wearing could be the last of my robes.
But as long as I have my peace, I can find relief.
Today could prove the most rewarding day of my life.
Today that very progress could suffer a backward slide.
But as long as I have my peace, I can find relief.
Despite whatever the challenge a day may bring,
It is mine to secure that measure of peace within.
For without my fill of peace, I may never find relief.
Central to all my priorities is securing my inner peace!

Pledge of Allegiance

This pledge, these words I say to you.
As spoken, such I have vowed to do.
And if at any point I am losing my way,
Remind me of the pledge without delay.
If I should bring tears to your eyes,
Then let me wipe away the stains.
And if I provoke you with smiles,
Permit me to do it over and again.
If I should find a place in your heart,
Then may you relax your inner fears.
And should I occupy your thoughts,
Then let it remind you that I care.
And if there is no music being heard,
Then may our laughter fill the room.
That even without the spoken word,
Our rhythmic silence will be attuned.
And for each time I hold your hand,
May you always feel safe and secure.
In that, you will always proudly stand
Each day taller than the day before.
If you should lose your will to fight,
Then let me help champion your cause.
That should there seem no end in sight,
I am there to help you bear your cross.
And if it is that we are growing apart,
Then let us uproot the bitter weeds
That on that day the harvest starts,
We will share a fill beyond our needs.
If I somehow lose my sense of place,
That I have fallen, help me get back up.

For I as well will have those days
That I will need that common touch.
And when in need of a companion,
Then let me be your listening ear.
If only for a firm place to stand on,
Then reach out to me; I will be there.
Whether there is a lack or overflow,
In whatever state, let us be content.
Notwithstanding, also learn to grow
That with each day, favor of strength.
If it seems we do no more but talk,
Then let us learn to communicate
That we may never starve the heart
And nourish the evils lying in wait.
This pledge I make, that I don't stray.
Above everything else, this much I ask,
That we be thankful for each given day,
And live each moment as if it is our last.

Race of Life

I am in the race of my life!
Each stage is a challenge to survive.
It is a grueling and demanding obstacle course.
It commands a very powerful and influential force.
It is as if I am running in an uninvited space.
More often than not, like I am out of place!

I am viewed as being least among all.
At any given moment, I am expected to fall.
The odds against me are continuously mounting
As if intent on shattering my confidence within.
Lined with a complexity of hurdles and stumbling blocks,
The course seems specifically designed to hold me back.

In this competitive race for my life,
I must fight twice as hard to stay alive.
Along this uneven, imbalanced track on which I run,
I must maintain my focus or forfeit my ground.
The loud and deafening cheers tell of deceptive tales.
This course is lined with many who hope I fail.

This is unlike any other race!
I have so much to prove if I am to earn my place.
The odds I am up against are stacked mountain high
As if aimed at limiting my ability to reach the sky.
Society has built imposing walls of exclusion zones,
Ever mindful, "Birds of a feather," "To each his own!"

Still, this is my absolute place!
I have earned every right to run in this race
Despite history's indelible scars and embedded pains.
Even so, I am no less of a man because I am stained.
On the contrary, they are more like stepping-stones,
They lay a firm foundation, so I can create my own.

As such, I will proudly run my own race!
I have mapped out the course and set my pace.
With each twist and turn along life's beaten path,
Determination and purpose are kept alive in my heart.
I face great odds, but victory is etched firmly in my mind.
Though I may fall along the way, I will not be left behind.

Rebound

I never thought it would hurt this much.
The disruption had caused me to sway.
Somehow it had disturbed my common touch.
My sense of balance was slipping away.
I was a victim of my own misguided choice.
A sudden fall from grace had subdued my voice.
I became consumed by my own foolish pride.
The many voices of reason I brushed aside.
In my quest to establish my own identity,
I dishonored the foundation they laid for me,
That circle with which I was then aligned.
I never saw that they, like me, were blind.
But in my haste to assert my individuality,
I failed to stop to consider what the costs may be.
There was a near tragic fall along a broken trail.
Then an eerie chill removed the winds from my sail.
But despite my near ill-fated fall from grace,
Somehow, I managed to maintain my sense of place.
For the voices of reason never left my side.
I marveled and then gutted my foolish pride.
I was knocked down but was never counted out.
My support structure had remained intact.
I lifted myself up in preparation for the bout.
There was a rebirth within; I was fighting back.
That which felled me had done so by deception.
There was an indelible stain on my integrity.
Still, a second chance for a first impression.
As if a rebranding, I was a new identity.
There was so much I had lost along the way.
Ever since the tragedy, the day that I first fell,

I considered the price I was forced to pay.
It was simply too costly to have to tell.
Each day brings progress by the rising of the sun.
In my heart there is a symphony of praise.
Informed, guided by purpose, I gradually rebound,
And I have since learned the error of my ways.

Remember

Remember the days!
Today it may seem like you are living a dream.
Then, at an instant, a disturbing, disruptive scene
For the scenes of life change ever so fast.
Remember the days!
As you steadily make your progressive strides,
Be mindful of the ones who stood by your side.
You could just be one step away from your past.
Remember!

Remember the words!
The value they hold will be revealed in time.
The words you ignore may become your lifeline,
The stones which the builders rejected!
Remember the words!
Life may not respond at once to your frantic call.
Be forewarned: A certain pride goes before a fall.
You may be found wanting when least expected.
Remember!

Remember the tears!
Love flows much slower when the hurt runs deep.
A heart may be reluctant to consider a repeat.
Life has no value when you are living alone.
Remember the tears!
Each one will have left an indelible stain.
Each one a reminder of the embedded pains.
Be mindful; tears have fears of their own.
Remember!

Remember the heart!
Guard and protect it, whatever the cost.
It could prove to be detrimental, a tragic loss.
Within, it holds the very essence of the man.
Remember the heart!
It is worth every measure of its weight in gold.
The heart of the man contains riches untold.
It is his foundation, that on which he stands.
Remember!

Remember the gift!
Life, a consideration granted by creation to man,
Favored with choice as part of the master plan.
One which only man in all of creation enjoys.
Remember the gift!
Man is the product of the choices he makes.
He is the author and finisher of his own fate.
The free will of choice is a very powerful voice.
Remember!

Resurrection

A second chance for a first impression!
The return of life, a resurrection!
A joy which my heart could barely contain.
I am breathing the breath of love again!
My heart opens up and takes it all in.
I have been resurrected; it is a new beginning!
In this, my hour of power, I smile with the sun.
Life tastes much sweeter the second time around.
I embrace its fullness, which is piercing through,
And in the midst of the experience, there was you.
You smiled with me; it was gentle and warm.
Then you reached out to me with wide-open arms.
It was as if for the first time, I felt safe and secure.
Your embrace embraced me; I was reassured.
Your touch humbled me, no words were spoken,
Quiet whispers of thoughts; my mind was open.
In the still of the moment, quieted with thoughts,
Emotions broke free and flooded my heart.
Alive again, the breath of love—a resurrection!
A second chance given to make a first impression.
To part ways with the old and start afresh, anew.
Another opportunity for a new beginning with you.
To live unrestrained and ignore self-imposed limits.
To love beyond borders and learn to grow with it.
To embrace the fullness of life and everything it gives,
Knowing that a life less appreciated is no life to live,
And that the breath of love is an open-heart affair.
To consider the brevity of life, that breath of air,
And to reach out to life while it is passing my way.
To be grateful for the favors it extends each day.

My soul is lifted; I am humbled by deep thoughts.
The fullness of life has returned to my heart.
In the still of the moment, I quietly take it all in.
I am favored with the privilege of a new beginning.
This, my second chance for a first impression!
Again, the breath of love, a resurrection!

Sacrifice

My finest moment, giving myself away!
For this, my world is beyond satisfied.
Abundance characterizes my mainstay.
I am highly favored with the favors of life,
To be champion for the cause of another.
Even the very thought excites—
That exercise of humility before honor,
Service above self, selflessness exercised!

The expression of humanity in motion!
To be concerned with that of another life.
It encourages inner growth and promotion
For life is larger than the sum of humankind.
The denial of self for an even greater cause.
There is no more considerate or noble act
In the spirit of humanity, reaching across.
One small step but with a lasting impact.

To be champion for someone else's cause.
To extend oneself beyond one's comfort zone.
In the name of humanity, the only reward
Driven by a purpose greater than his own.
Helplessness, on the opposite side of life;
It is a place where no man should ever be.
To give of oneself in the spirit of sacrifice.
It expresses an appreciation for humanity.

Selflessness: That campaign for humanity!
A compassionate touch, bridging the divide,
To so extend oneself as if ordained duty,
The most potent deed for the sanctity of life.
No man is indeed an island onto himself;
Each is an individual link in the human chain
To be champion for the cause for someone else.
Sacrifice tells of untold and incalculable gains.

Sacrifice: An exercise of humanity in motion.
Selflessness: A compassionate brother in arms,
Bonded together, a pledge of self with devotion.
Denying self, reaching out simply just because.
Out of the humility and lowliness of the heart.
Angels lie in wait, ever willing champions for life.
A small act for humanity, a ray of light in the dark.
In life, nothing is more rewarding than sacrifice.

Sing

I will continually sing!
Despite whatever the day may bring,
I will not overwhelm this heart!
It has faithfully borne me from the start.
Today I am favored with the privilege of the gift.
This moment is the only certainty I have with it
And consider it to be my one certain breath.
So I will breathe it with little to no regrets.
As long as I enjoy the breath of life, I will sing.
I will sing despite the challenges the day may bring,
Though mindful there are trials on each given day.
And obstacles will surface at an instant along the way;
Some may indeed overwhelm or even silence the voice.
Even so, as long as I live, I will make a joyful noise
For life never promised that it would be a bed of roses.
Instead, that one door stands open as another one closes.
There is nothing in life that is ever completely absolute.
Encouraged by the Word, I embrace the proven truth.
So notwithstanding whatever the day may bring.
As many hours in the day are as many there are to sing.
Even if I am brought to my knees, I will sing in defiance.
The silence of my voice doesn't mean my voice is silenced.
Even if bombarded by chatter, I will make a joyful noise.
By singing, the enemy will know that I still have a voice,
And those weapons formed against me, intending to win,
By the power which is vested in me, I will continuously sing.
I will not overwhelm my heart with any needless weight.
There is only a certain measure that it was designed to take.
Even more reason to sing; the battle before me is not mine!
It is that of he who watches over me, the protector of my life.

So, despite whatever clever devices the enemy may have laid,
I will sing! For my heart will neither be troubled nor afraid.
I will sing and make a joyful noise so all the world may hear!
I will sing and make a joyful noise for it is a thankful affair!
I will sing so that the enemies may know I am still alive!
I will make a joyful noise while ten thousand fall by my side!
No weapon formed against me shall ever silence my voice.
No burden so overwhelming that my heart can never rejoice.
Though life does have its trials, as is evident each given day,
It also comes with sufficient grace to guide us along the way.
Life is an amazing gift; its wonders never cease!
It transcends the imagination in its ever-changing scenes.
Despite whatever the challenge, the greater power is within.
Life, being an amazing gift of grace, is reason enough to sing.

Sometimes

Sometimes,
While doing a mental audit at the end of the day,
A review of the many activities done along the way,
Every so often I break into a smile.
It is such a beautiful gift, life!
Looking over all the profits and losses,
An analysis of the various reasons and causes,
As I consider the bounty which remains,
I question the need for man to complain.
Sometimes.

Sometimes,
In a search for answers that make sense of it all,
After I would have suffered an unexpected fall,
Then it would later dawn on me
How blessed and highly favored I must be!
It became evident after a careful inspection
Out in the open, following deep introspection,
Despite how well planned your day may be,
There will be interruptions unsuspectingly.
Sometimes.

Sometimes,
Because of the speed in which we live our lives,
We fail to appreciate the very essence of life.
Consider the needless price we often pay!
Living life in the moment is fading away.
Life is indeed a precious and amazing gift.
Its value comes from whatever we make of it.
We lose so much through our wanton haste.
If only we learn to adjust our blistering pace!

Sometimes.

Sometimes,
I marvel at man's level of communication.
Man, superior in intelligence in all of creation,
Yet every so often, he never ceases to amaze me.
I am particularly amused at the calamity.
Emotions sink deep, like a weight in my heart.
My inner sense of balance is upset by thoughts.
My hope is that man breaks his injurious spell;
That he makes the time to reconnect with himself.
Sometimes.

SOS

This is a message from Mother Earth to man: "SOS!"
Please pay special attention to my signals of distress.
Of the highest importance, this is for all of humankind.
The situation is critical; there are many warning signs.
Take the necessary steps now, or it may just be too late.
If you cross that dividing line, it could seal our fates.
At this current rate, you are going to crash and burn.
You are nearing critical mass, the point of no return.

Without me, it is just impossible for you to survive.
Your basic and all needed essentials of life I provide.
Even a fresh supply of the very air that you breathe.
I am the one you must rely on for all that you need.
If only you could somehow experience the pains!
Perhaps then, my concerns would not echo in vain.
Your lack of care is upsetting, and the hurt runs deep.
I try to be strong, but your attitude is making me weak.

Time and again, I reminisce about the days of long ago.
Then, even the heavens marveled at this beauty below.
I was the pride of creation; I was purposely designed.
I was spirited and vibrant and filled with abundant life.
I was a mist of fresh air, simply unparalleled and pristine.
Also, an amazement of wonder, a marvel of a scene.
A picture of perfection, I was the heart of the master plan.
I was complete and self-sustaining. Then there was man!

With each passing day, I break down with teary eyes.
It is so troubling just to look at the once clear blue skies.
The sun burns through my face with an unbearable heat.
I am left bare and exposed, while you take shelter in retreat.
Your reckless endangerment has now scarred my perfection.
By destroying my shield, I am now left with little protection.
The once fresh air is so toxic I am slowly losing my breath.
I can hardly breathe; it is suffocating; I am choking to death.

There was a time I was very warm and tender to the touch.
But the extremes of the weather are now proving too much.
And when I am thirsty and in need of a cool, refreshing drink,
The water has become so heavy that my heart painfully sinks.
There is an unsettling sensation that runs through my veins.
The clouds told on you; the poisonous substance is acid rain.
Your advances have left a negative impact on my temperature.
The fallout is disturbing; I am becoming meaner than ever.

It is my hope that you acknowledge my SOS.
We both must work together to address this urgent mess.
Although critical, it is salvageable; we still have some time.
But we need to start now in order to avoid crossing that line.
Your rapid development is costing us both quite a hefty price,
Considering I have become the lamb being unfairly sacrificed.
While I applaud your advances, your growth, and development,
Consider the impact it is having on both of our environments.

Take the Music

Take the music …
The favor of life has blessed you with it.
Take the music, go out, and light your world.
All the world is a stage; life is your open door.
The music is the winds beneath your wings; soar.
Take the music and play your life undisturbed.
Take the music …

Take the music …
The power is in your hands, so use it.
Master your craft, create your own work of art,
Play whatever selections you choose to hear.
String your own chords; it is a personal affair.
Take the music and play it from your heart.
Take the music …

Take the music …
Yours is special and unique; don't lose it.
Play beyond borders; be as free as the winds.
Yours is not restricted by boundaries or reach.
It is your voice; express your freedom of speech.
The greatest of your power lives deep within.
Take the music …

Take the music …
It is your gateway to life, so choose it.
All of life is before you; it is an open door.
The pathways to the favors of life are all yours.
Choose your rhythms, select your own chords,
Fill the heavens with music never heard before.

Take the music …

Take the music …
The fullness of life will promote you through it.
The spirit of your mind is where it all begins.
Embrace the music, play it with an open heart,
Create your masterpiece, your own work of art.
Become one with the music; open and let it in.
Take the music …

Take the music …
The favor of life has blessed you through it,
Take the music, go out, and change the world.
The music is your seed to a bountiful life, sow.
It has an abundance of favors to help you grow.
Take the music; your place has been reserved.
Take the music …

The Bond of Love

Love is the structure of life!
Life is the foundation that keeps the structure alive.
Together, they are like an orchestrated symphony,
One accompanying the other in harmony.
With a unity of purpose, the two became as one.
With a common interest, they forged a special bond,
Two individual forces, each unique in personality,
United for a common cause into a single entity.
Over the process of time, they come to discover
That none on its own can survive without the other.
The bond has championed the call for renewed focus—
The birth of a new beginning, a spirit of trust.
Love cultivated the seeds of hope.
Life reciprocated with explosive growth.
By uncluttering its heart, which was a desolate place,
Life began to see real value in its once-guarded space.
Then it was dense and secured, a heavily protected lot.
All previous attempts of entry were successfully blocked.
It suffered a decrease in value from lack of upkeep and care.
Then a decline in investment as new interests disappeared.
But behind the new winds of change that came blowing in,
A very powerful alliance was lurking in the winds.
Unlimited in potential, each in their own individual right,
But a force to be reckoned with when they join forces, unite.
Life and love embraced each other with an open mind.
Theirs was no chance encounter; it was purposed by design.
Love promoted life with a new attitude.
The old ways of life were discarded and then renewed.
Bonded and balanced, as if like spirited little children.
Inseparable, they have since become the best of friends.

Love lifted life with hope; it added value and purpose.
There was mutual understanding, a foundation of trust.
Life welcomed love with a wide-open embrace.
Commitment and direction boosted their sense of place.
Structured and centered, they have both risen above,
Each contributing to the cause in the bond of love.

The Duel

This is a battle of wills; it is a fight for supremacy.
When the dust settles, one of us will be no more.
This battle is for the ultimate prize, for a legacy.
This, the decisive duel, will at last settle the score.
Indeed, we are both accomplished men of valor.
Each a champion in his own right and class.
This duel will finally herald a legitimacy of honor.
This is the ultimate battle, and it will be our last.

We are each a celebrated warrior in our individual right.
Each tower like giants on the ground where he stands.
Rivals sharing the same space in the same spotlight,
More so in a space which was solely reserved for one.
Yes, we are both decorated by the weight of our names,
And we each demonstrate a measure of mutual respect.
And though both men of valor, each has different aims.
I am a champion for life, but yours is worse than death.

You are undoubtedly a very cunning and deceitful foe,
And I acknowledge the reason many call you "Fear."
Crafty, your invasion into the mind, disrupting its flow,
Such that you have become the dominant voice it hears.
One might admit that it is quite an impressive strategy,
Considering that the mind is the seat of control of man.
But impressive and tactful as your approach might be,
By observing you closely, I have developed a plan.

I commend your sense of discipline and determination.
I am encouraged as well by your relentless quest to win.
But there is a stronger will, far beyond your imagination.
That of the human spirit; it is that which empowers him.
Indeed, you are very clever; you study your subjects well.
The records reflect that you have accomplished very much.
Your plunders are all clearly evident, the many you felled.
But there are minds that you cannot break or even disrupt.

Undoubtedly, you command a crafty and powerful force.
Your many spoils of wars are paraded openly each day.
But this mind which stands before you, the power it holds!
It can match you at whatever level; it is no wounded prey.
Those weapons of your warfare are all mental by design;
You are as that clever enemy who plants the corrupt weed.
But your weapons can never conquer the spirit of this mind
Armed with the human will, it is the only weapon that I need.

Today, clash of the champions, the ultimate showdown,
Today the moment of truth is set to unravel, unfold.
The day which I have longed waited for has finally come.
Ours will be the ultimate battle, the battle for control.
There is an age-old question, from the days of long ago
About an irresistible force up against an immovable object.
Curious and enquiring minds have always wanted to know
So, today we will give them their greatest understanding yet.

The mother of all duels, before the masses, for all to see,
Played out on life's grand stage, the battle set for one fall.
It will be a no holds barred affair between you and me
And when the bell finally rings, the winner will take all.
This is a high stakes encounter; legacies are on the line.
That you will come at me full force, I expect nothing less.
The spirit of fear in battle against the spirit of the mind
Today, every and all misconceptions will be laid to rest.

The Enemy Within

This I hold to be true from the bottom of my heart,
That man was the image of perfection at the very start.
And with the greatest of all purposes in mind!
Control, from the beginning, in his hands by design,
But as he increased in knowledge with each passing day,
By choice, he ignored the rules somewhere along the way.
And fed by his curious nature, he has been sadly deposed.
Now, man in a fight against himself on a collision course.

The genius of man is seated at his core, deep within.
He holds much greater potential than he can ever imagine.
The mind of man is a hoarding of unlimited power,
A treasure trove of wealth lying in wait to be discovered.
Consider the extent of the knowledge he has already honed!
Imagine the potential as he advances toward the unknown!
Man must be complimented on what he has already achieved.
Undeniably, nothing is impossible for him who believes!

The mind of man is truly a powerful and amazing thing.
He has proven he can accomplish such as he imagines.
Indeed, a highly creative being, man is pure visionary.
There is little that the mind of man is unable to see or be.
Although fully aware that there are natural limitations.
Even so, yet undaunted, he engages the power of imagination.
He is encouraged by his successes, such as he has overcome.
He is driven by his advances, the great things he has done.

But it is evident that man is becoming hopelessly dependent.
He has unwittingly subjected himself to his crafty inventions.
And by his dependence on the world his very hands have made,
Unintentionally he has turned himself into a virtual slave
By extending the wings of his imagination to soar in flight,
By stretching his level of curiosity to ever progressive heights.
Control becoming secondary to his growing, insatiable quests,
Man has become an unintended victim of his own success.

Today, it is virtually impossible for him to turn it about.
His has become a world with which he can never do without.
Man is so deeply connected to his notable accomplishments
That he is now a technical by-product of his own development.
And as the explosion of knowledge continues to unfold,
The greatest of his challenges will be to maintain control.
By being driven and unrelenting to feed that beast deep in him,
Man has yet to demonstrate control over the enemy within.

The Heart of Survival

A masterpiece of creation, created perfect from the start,
Man is an unparalleled and incomparable work of art.
Without question, simply genius, the pride of creation.
That of a superior wisdom, an unfathomable imagination.
Whatever may be the challenges he is forced to confront,
Man has the potential and creativity within to overcome.
Only by subjecting to fear he allows obstacles to limit him.
Considering his creative genius, he is as his mind imagines.

Man is the product of all the choices he makes.
More so, he is the sole author and finisher of his own fate.
The mind is itself pure mastery—indeed, an amazing thing.
But it is the heart which tells of the essence of man within.
Man lives by a certain code, as he wholeheartedly believes.
Such is one of his most definitive and distinct qualities.
Prone to self-preservation, his natural impulse is to survive.
He relies on whatever is at his disposal in order to stay alive.

Highly favored by creation, that which has set him apart,
Being conscious of his disposition, he lives within his heart.
Ever mindful of his position, a privileged place, by himself,
Heralded the pride of creation, rising above everything else.
Whenever challenged by challenges, even by fear and doubt,
Resource filled, he employs as needed to direct his way out.
Courage coming under fire is threatening to his sense of place.
He draws on his resources in defense of his personal space.

A highly sensitive creature, man is a hotbed of emotions.
When engaged, he instinctively reacts as fluid as the ocean.
At times he opts for retreat, a convenient weapon of choice.
It affords him a tactical advantage; silence is a powerful voice.
A master at adaptation, a strategy employed in defense of self.
That the heart feeds itself first, it enjoys priority above all else.
Any threats of imposition or a disruption of his normal state,
Forced by circumstances, he responds as may seem appropriate.

To safeguard the integrity of the bounty he holds in his heart,
He activates protective measures; man is masterful at the art.
The expansive plains of life represent a shady and crafty place.
Being a master of deception, the enemy could be a familiar face.
Complacency, or a loss in focus, could signal his tragic demise.
Man must maintain the integrity of the heart in order to survive.
Notwithstanding, the enemy is relentless, and as each day unfolds,
Man's greatest challenge lies within that of a discipline of control.

The Match

Had it not been for that bell!
It seemed I was doing so well!
My confidence was never higher.
My adrenaline raged like a fire.
Mine seemed to be the advantage.
I was inflicting serious damage.
I was writing my personal story.
I was shaping my place in history.

The spectators were so animated.
They were very vocal and elated.
Everything was going just right.
Winning seemed to be in sight.
As if I was on top of a pinnacle,
My performance was a spectacle.
It was if all was going in my favor.
The thrill of victory I began to savor.

But as I would soon come to learn,
Life is a maze of unpredicted turns.
The mind holds remarkable powers.
This I would later come to discover.
Time and again it is underestimated,
Its powers miscounted, miscalculated.
But it possesses the will to vary a course—
Limitless potential, invaluable resource!

Consumed by my own inner strength,
I was up against the wrong opponent.
It was then I had come to understand,
At that very instant, I became a man.
The more they chanted and cheered,
Even the further I retreated with fear.
Soon I would lose all sight of the goal.
Somehow, I was slowly losing control.

In the end, it was pure wasted energy.
The opponent I was fighting was me.
Lifted by the strengths that I possessed,
As if it was all needed to achieve success.
But amid the jubilation I heard a call,
A voice echoed, "Pride goes before a fall!"
I lay there in astonishment on the floor.
I had never been beaten by myself before!

The Prayer

Last night as you prayed, I heard.
I listened intently to your every word.
As I lay in the dark beside myself in my room,
In an instant, it was as if I felt something moved.
There was heaviness in my heart.
I was frozen in place; I was falling apart.
My spirit was troubled, and I sensed a worrying fear,
As if being convicted by the words of the prayer.
The words deeply touched me.
It was as if they were conducting a search of me.
But as the prayer continued,
I felt an unusual calm in the room.
Tears were settled in my eyes.
I was down on my knees before I realized.
I was quietly drowning in pain.
The trials of life were driving me insane.
The doors to my heart were tightly closed.
But somehow they opened; I was then exposed.
There was like a great battle deep within
For I was fighting the invader with everything.
I resisted as best as I could with all my might,
But a greater power took control of me last night.
It easily broke through my defenses.
It humbled me and connected me to my senses.
Even so, I felt as if I was somehow deceived
For I was never known to be one who believed.
Then there was an air of deafening silence.
I thought I had won with my relentless defiance.
But that wasn't to be, as I later became aware.
On my knees, the silence was a whispering prayer.

Unwittingly, I quietly poured my heavy heart out.
The words flowed freely as I opened my mouth.
And as I emptied my heart in a great outpour,
There was a relief such as never experienced before.
I paused for a moment to collect my thoughts.
A quieting peace settled deep in my heart.
And then it was as if almost immediately
I felt as though there was a new man in me.
It was as if I was granted a renewed lease on life.
A new sense of purpose had filled me inside.
And at that very instant, an uplifting thrill.
The whisper of a voice said, "Peace, be still!"
There was a quiet surrender and then a new joy within.
It opened wide its heart and welcomed me in.
I lifted myself up with a warm smile on my face.
A transformation had miraculously taken place.
I am so relieved to have been there!
And even more excited I heard your prayer.
Once I was lost, but now I have found my way.
I found it the very hour I took the time to pray.

The Promise

A new wind of change, new air to breathe!
The change which we longed for indeed!
For the many years we were forced to stand down,
A new light of hope has finally come.
Out of the murky shadows it appears.
The myths of the dark ages have disappeared.
Today, our faith has been restored.
We will not be silent anymore!
With a unity of purpose, our voices have spoken.
The chains of suppression are finally broken.
A new era is born!
The dream lives on!
It is the birth of a new age,
A timely and welcomed wind of change.
Though voices of past struggles were crudely silenced,
They echo from their graves with daring defiance.
Today, their dream lives on.
Today breaks a new dawn.
Change has found a new face.
It has been warmly embraced,
Though many attempted to stain its integrity.
Yet the world was humbled by its humility.
It tells of the measure of the man.
He empowers, "Yes, we can!"
A man humbly made in the heart;
It has set him apart!
A new era is revealing.
It is a promise of hope, resurrection, and healing.
And because our painful hearts sorely remember,
We will never again either retreat or surrender

For the flames of hope again burn bright.
Finally, we have seen the light!
Today, ours is an identity beyond a mere existence.
One mind, one voice can make a difference!

The Reckoning

Long ago, someone senselessly died by my hands.
Today, I am still at a loss to grasp it, understand.
Every so often, that day repeatedly plays back.
To date, I find no answers for the insensitive act.
I was in a daze as he lay motionless on the ground.
Unprovoked, I had no explanation for what I'd done.
With a disturbed sense of balance, I neared the line.
The man who died was a very close friend of mine.

With each passing day, as reality gradually unfolds,
The impact of the tragedy quietly took its toll.
As the events of that fateful day played back in my head,
I thought, *it should have been me who died instead!*
It was if an invading force had taken possession of me.
There was no justifiable explanation for the tragedy.
Despite the pains which resulted from innocence lost,
My heart won't forgive me or display any remorse.

Gradually, as the process of time quietly drifts away,
I am haunted by recurring images of that fateful day.
Time and again, recurrent eruptions of internal rage.
But the explosions are restricted within my mental cage.
They have proven virtually impossible for me to defeat.
Mine had since become endless nights of restless sleep.
In my mind, the events of that day play back repeatedly.
There are frequent and grim reminders of the tragedy.

The effect of the tragedy has disturbed my sense of place.
The memories of our friendship are impossible to erase.
Echoes of spirited, playful voices move me to silent tears.
In the still of the moment, they whisper loudly in my ears.
But even as the disruptive images graphically unfold,
The effects of that tragic day have already taken their toll.
Although the heart tries encouraging itself to remain strong,
Reality has proven time and again that it won't be for long.

I have been reduced to less than a man since that fateful day.
Within these solitary confines, I am gradually wasting away.
As I wrestle with the grave consequences of the tragedy,
I have since become less than the man I once used to be.
Many a heart attempt to reassure and comfort me in embrace,
But even those very gestures offer little reparation or solace.
Broken and tormented, with no real purpose under the sun,
Death would have been more welcome as my final outcome.

The Rumor

The rumor, it spread like a wild fire!
Curious minds excitedly inquired.
Whispers hissed in the dark.
The toxic details fueled a disastrous spark.
As if like sweet music to the ears,
Laughter exploded with joyous cheers.
It circulated like hot breaking news.
There was no shortage of gossip and views.

As the buzz of words increased, intensified,
The environment became more electrified.
Eyes lit up with wide-open stares.
Unbelief permeated the atmosphere.
This was seemingly no ordinary rumor!
Hearts burst open with explosive humor.
Sarcasm and ridicule rose to new heights.
Disgust boldly expressed itself in delight.

Around every block and street corner,
Across the open plains and distant borders,
Like the far-reaching effects of an epidemic,
Virtually every ear had been infected with it.
Though it was only a rumor and bore no proof,
There were changes in relations and attitudes.
Even worse, treated as if like a social outcast,
Scorned and despised like a leper in times past.

This rumor simply had to be true!
All seemed to share the same point of view.
But the consequences of baseless allegations!
Innocence brought down by character assassination.
Sadly, a harrowing case of mischief and enmity!
Then a senseless attack on an innocent personality.
It ripped through a heart with unconscionable pain.
Few dared to stop and question the unfounded claim.

Still, amid the malicious chatter of words,
A total lack of consideration for the resulting hurt.
Yet an innocent life was deliberately brought down
By the poison of a mischievous and envious tongue.
But in due course, as long as time sets the stage,
All unfair games will eventually be replayed.
And after the dust has settled and cleared,
That which life rewards will be that which is fair.

The Season of Life

Life continues marching on
Long after the laughter is gone
And a vacuum has settled in place.
The heart must remain strong
Even though the tears may come
And the memories seem hard to erase.

Indeed, the sting is hard to bear.
The loss is a painful, disruptive affair.
The hiss of death is beyond man's control.
At such a time, there is no transfer of pain;
Others can only imagine but in vain,
Though the words try their best to console.

Still, in their own unique way,
The peculiar role that memories play!
Recalling special moments from the past,
Providing a temporary relief from the pain.
You are able to smile that way again,
But only for as long as the memories last.

And so, life will continue on.
And with tomorrow comes a new dawn.
Fresh new challenges to face up ahead.
Life owes none of us any reason.
For everything there is a season.
So, embrace life for the present instead.

All of life is a repetitive cycle.
What was then is now, all in a circle.
Nothing that happens is new under the sun.
All of life is the work of a superior will,
And according to order, it must be fulfilled.
The same decides when the season of life is done.

The Song

Genius at play, a beautifully written song,
A masterpiece, an amazing work of art.
Today, now my closest friend and companion,
It has secured a special place in my heart.
We made a connection from the very first day.
Like a best friend, it is always on my mind.
Wherever I may be and the song begins to play,
I just sit back, let go, and simply unwind.
The song accompanies me wherever I go.
Like a shadow, it never leaves my side.
We two have since become inseparable.
It is like that voice within, my daily guide.
Its words find their place deep within my soul.
They are like that inner voice I depend on.
Whenever the song plays, it assumes control.
It receives my complete and undivided attention.
Whenever lost, confused, or can't find my way,
When emotion blinds reason or I am in doubt,
It is at such moments the song begins to play.
It quiets me and then directs my way out.
At times, it breaks through my core defenses.
Then I become as if an open door.
But by exposing my strengths and my weaknesses,
It reveals things I had never seen before.
The song is my life, and it lives deep within.
Its words excite that spirit of hope.
It is that inner voice which beautifully sings.
Deep rooted, it reassures and encourages growth.
The song has provided me with a comfort zone.
It has become a proven and very trusted friend.

I am reassured by the promise that I am never alone,
That it will stand by me through the very end.
As each day goes by, I carefully learn the song.
It has become a particular favorite of mine.
We two have established an unbreakable bond.
It plays a very active role in my life.
It is not only my secret place but also a retreat
For there are moments when life does overwhelm.
It rallies support for me against the agony of defeat.
The thrill of victory is its close ally and friend.

The Vigilante Diaries

I once lived a notorious life of crime.
But I have paid my dues; I've done my time.
I promised myself to walk the narrow way,
Turned my back on the man I was yesterday.
No longer a menacing threat to the society,
There was a rehabilitation of the mind in me.
As well, I had rid myself of that infamous name.
I had gotten my full share of notoriety and fame.

Everything that gave me purpose and identity,
Those to whom I was obligated, my family—
The hands of crime senselessly took them all.
And ultimately, it resulted in my spiraled fall.
The system of the day failed to bring me closure.
As such, I became a shadow so as to avoid exposure.
I became a vigilante, an angel of death in disguise.
But somehow, I was granted a renewed lease on life.

Those of my inner circle, the ones who knew me,
They are proud of the man I turned out to be.
While in dark isolation, I turned my focus around.
Granted this new lease on life, I was on the rebound.
But the journey was no easy Sunday afternoon walk.
The exercise of adjustment was the challenging part.
I wrestled hard against the temptation of going back.
A fight between me and my past, daily under attack.

With each passing day, I was making steady progress.
I got engaged in the activities that I loved doing best.
I was intent on walking away from that menacing past.
But the world which surrounded me changed ever so fast.
Considering I had no fixed place of habitation or abode,
Nor any social or personal obligations of my own,
Every so often, I considered it necessary to relocate
In order that certain past triggers would not reactivate.

But life seemed against me; I was fast losing control.
This transformation effort was slowly taking its toll.
Flashing and haunting images of the years of long ago,
Invasive and protruding, they were disrupting the flow.
Certain images taunted me; they proved hard to escape.
Triggers I tried avoiding, which upset my mental state.
Invading my personal space, echoes of desperate cries.
And like a moth to the flames, out of the shadows I rise.

It was a daunting exercise; I was being put to the test.
Reluctantly, I returned to the man I was known for best.
Patient-in-waiting, soft-spoken, seemingly undisturbed.
This is the mode by which my life had proven its worth.
Those who preyed on the weak fell into my line of sight.
Mine was a solo campaign against the evils of the night.
A shady figure in the shadows, oblivious of society's laws,
Once again that masked avenger with a menacing cause.

Timeless Beauty

She is a vision of timeless beauty
As if preserved by the hands of time,
An unfailing progression, continuity.
She was created flawlessly by design,
Pleasing to the eyes, birthed in desire.
Her scent of attraction lures, endears,
As the inner cravings ignite like a fire.
Yet fragile, she must be handled with care.

She is a pillar of timeless beauty.
She brings stability and value to life.
Her place must not be treated loosely.
Balance and security stand at her side.
Like darkness pierced by a ray of light,
She is charged by the flicker of the sun.
The power of her touch awakes, excites.
The strength of her power overcomes.

She is a figure of timeless beauty.
There is none who can take her place.
Her weight speaks to a sense of duty.
She stands with dignity, even grace.
Despite a being of sensuous pleasure,
She is the wind which gives lift to life.
To soar without limits, above measure,
Her sense of place can never be denied.

She is a beam of timeless beauty,
A radiance, as if reflecting the sun,
Penetrating at will and with impunity.
Her presence tells that victory is won,
That ray of light illuminating the heart.
Hers is a touch that can never grow cold.
Her position in life was a careful thought,
And her weight is far beyond that of gold.

She is the essence of timeless beauty.
Without her, life is mere empty space.
Complete and entire, purpose and unity,
All of creation is influenced by her grace.
Essential to growth, hers is a balancing act.
She brings fulfillment to the order of things.
Fullness, a bounty, even in the face of lack.
She is like the winds beneath life's wings.

She is an expression of timeless beauty.
Her voice echoes in silence, yet assertive.
When enraged, even hell can feel her fury.
And life's storms, obedient and submissive,
For she occupies a very commanding space.
Purposed by creation, an ordered duty of care,
There is none other who can take her place.
Timeless beauty, it tells of a permanent affair.

Today

Today I smiled!
I am still highly favored by life.
Every challenge that has come my way
Only served to strengthen me today.
Considering that life is on my side,
Today I am able to smile!

Today I found my peace!
It came after I learned to release
The heavy burdens I carried around.
They did no more but kept me down.
But a renewing of the mind, relief.
Today I found my peace!

Today I uncovered my strengths!
Now I am rebuilding with confidence.
Fears and doubts had invaded my mind.
Overwhelmed, I eventually fell behind.
Nonetheless, courage became my friend.
Today I uncovered my strengths!

Today I am a pillar of hope!
I am lifted with the spirit of growth.
My mind had become a terrible waste.
Such as enjoyed, gone without a trace.
But encouraging was the voice which spoke.
Today I am a pillar of hope!

Today I made that break!
Empowered, I took a leap of faith.
I stepped beyond my comfort zone.
My fears became my stepping-stones.
The thrill of victory was lying in wait.
Today I made that break!

Today I smiled!
Today I am still the favor of life.
I am highly favored, richly blessed.
Though undeserving, nonetheless,
The many favors of life are still mine.
Today I am able to smile!

Tomorrow

Tomorrow …
The border between the present and an uncharted time zone,
A journey into a dark territory, into the unknown.
Like that of a mystical land, heard of but is never seen,
An imagined world of expectation but in reality, a dream.
It is where hope finds its solace and life procrastinates.
The place where life finds its release, its avenue of escape.
Life's retreat from the present, when circumstances overwhelm,
Transporting the cares of the moment over into another realm.
It provides a temporary relief from the immediacies of life.
It is designed as a bay of refuge, a shelter from life's rising tides.

Tomorrow …
At the edge of the day, the other end of the spectrum,
In just one sleep and a wake, and then reality comes.
That dark cloud which blinded vision after it goes away.
Among the strangest ironies of life, tomorrow is today!
In the constancy of time, at that instant, the very moment
In life's natural progression, it is the only door which is open.
Tomorrow is today; the changing scenes of life change fast.
For every minute which life gives, in a second, it is past.
Tomorrow is virtual reality; it is a mere figment of the mind.
Tomorrow is today in motion but a little further down the line.

Tomorrow …
With the breaking of dawn, daylight follows closely behind.
That new page which is turned contains its own rule of lines.
Despite life's changing scenes, time continues without delay.
It tells of the plain realities of life; tomorrow is in fact today.
Life is no respecter of person, even for who may be unprepared.
In its natural progression, the journey of life is a readiness affair.
To actively promote a cause for tomorrow at the expense of today
Could prove counterproductive to gains made along the way.
Tomorrow is a miscalculation of the value and measure of time.
It represents a miscarriage of thought; it is a product of the mind.

Tomorrow …
The course which is set will be complete, and then all will be ended.
Its breath will be expired, its many opportunities gone, expended.
Or perhaps then the mind will open as reality passes by its way.
For even that of one thousand years is but for tomorrow a day.
Then the mind may see the beauty of life, its eyes being wide open,
And realize that the essence of the gift is to savor the given moment.
For not even tomorrow can consider the measure of its own breath.
Today is, and will undoubtedly be, tomorrow's most valuable asset.

Tomorrow …
At the furthest reach of the present, along the ridgeline,
Positioned just beyond the horizon, and advancing like time,
In the natural order of things, with all being said and done,
In life's natural progression, tomorrow—in reality—never comes.
The process of time is constant; it neither pauses nor does it wait.
It holds no respect for person or consideration for any mental state.
No man, or even life itself, can intimate what tomorrow is going to be.
In like manner, neither can tomorrow offer an assurance or guarantee.
The only surety in life is the present; tomorrow is but one breath away.
In life, there is no such as tomorrow because tomorrow is in fact today.

When Darkness Falls

When darkness falls,
When the light of day has been recalled,
As life gradually reduces its hurried pace,
Orderly, the changing of the guards takes place.
And as the daylight gracefully steps aside,
There is a moving display; it amazes, delights.
A colorful fanfare at the changing of the guards,
A demonstration of honor as daylight departs
When darkness falls.

When darkness falls,
The dusk announces its arrival to all
In the heavens above and on earth beneath.
All of life is impacted when it takes its seat.
And as it begins its role as guardian of the night,
Following the transfer with the receding light,
The power of its touch tells of a restorative calm.
All of life becomes battered by a quiet storm
When darkness falls.

When darkness falls,
The sounds of the night are as a noisome brawl.
The critters of the night blast with a musical rage.
And until the break of dawn, all the world is a stage
As life becomes enthralled by this musical treat,
As it unwinds and fuses with the rhythmic beats.
The heart is lifted, its myriad cares set aside,
Moved by the melodies of the music of the night
When darkness falls.

When darkness falls,
In the still of the moment, life reminisces, recalls.
An invasion of thoughts opens communication lines.
There is a quiet introspection, a meeting of minds.
And during the discourse, many clutters get cleared.
The engaging exchange becomes a healing affair.
Deep inhales and exhales lead a gradual release.
As the healing continues, the heart holds its peace
When darkness falls.

When darkness falls,
The ears become tuned to every whisper of a call.
Echoes in the distance befriend the passing breeze.
Frolicking waves display the calmer side of the seas.
And as the onslaught of peace establishes its control,
As the music of the night quietly penetrates the soul,
The spirit of man sighs in quiet reverence and praise.
All as the renewing of the mind serenely takes place
When darkness falls.

Winner by Design

Run your own race!
Run at your own pace!
The outcome is yours to choose.
You decide, win or lose.
Even if you are just a beginner,
Decide you want to be a winner.
But once at the starting line,
Begin with the end in mind.
Winners know failing is not the enemy.
Instead, it is a stepping-stone to destiny.
Failing and failure are not the same;
Failure must never be entertained.
Winners seize their moments in time.
Winners win in attitudes and minds.
A winner is never afraid to fail.
Winners pay close attention to detail.
They know their weaknesses and strengths.
Winners continuously work on themselves.
A winner chooses to become a winner.
Anything less will never be considered.
Winners create their own outlines.
Winners become winners by design.
Winners are not contained within their shells.
They extend outward, beyond themselves.
Winners are never opposed to change;
Such is even encouraged and embraced.
Winners associate with their own kind
But pave clear paths for those behind.
A winner always competes against himself.
His is self-growth, a standard of excellence.

A winner chooses to win by design.
The path to winning begins in his mind.
A winner leads by his own example.
A winner becomes his greatest role model.
The circle of life is continuously spinning;
Each day tests his resolve to keep on winning.
Even the greatest of winners sometimes fall,
But daily reconditioning is key to standing tall.
Winning is a discipline of attitude and mind.
Winning is not accidental but purpose-defined.
Winning takes character and constant effort,
Ever fostering inner growth to keep growing up
For in life, seasons come and seasons go.
A winner by design requires a will to always sow.
The spirit of winning is in the soul of every man.
The direction of growth takes root where he stands.
Obstacles will surface on the rise toward the top.
The discipline of sacrifice will ensure he never stops.
But only if he wants it, if it is purposed in the mind;
It takes work to become a winner, a winner by design.

Words

Consider the infinite power of words!
That which they possess deep inside,
Contained within themselves yet reserved.
They were the power which gave birth to life.
There is no power on earth which compares.
They occupy a fixed and unshakeable space
Of a godlike nature, omnipresent, everywhere.
The presence of man gives them a lasting place.

Consider the imaginative genius of words!
Imagine life without the proficiency of such.
Their place is firmly established, undisturbed.
The whole of life is influenced by their touch.
There is no barrier which can block their paths.
Words command an artful, dexterous force.
Resource-oriented, they enjoy a dynamic walk.
No power on earth is able to alter their course.

Consider the creative mastery of words!
Their wisdom leads the development of man.
The voice of their power speaks boldly, unstirred.
The power of their voice enjoys an enduring stand.
Even a physical impairment cannot limit their reach.
Their superior wisdom tells of profound mastery.
Even the whisper of a thought is a powerful speech.
Being ever resilient, they exercise bold impunity.

Consider the deep impact of words!
Like a bridge, they provide a firm foundation.
Transcending borders, they advance undeterred.
They open the gateway to communication.
They occupy a fundamental and critical space.
They command a strategic and vital ground.
There is nothing as essential that can take their place.
Being translated, they speak fluently in every tongue.

Consider the character of words!
Centered, a true reflection of their roots.
As disciplined and cultured, so they preserve.
Whatever the weather, they consistently bear fruit.
By their very nature, every expression precedes a cause.
Driven by purpose, they express themselves openly,
Though the words spoken may expose character flaws.
Nevertheless, the spoken words communicate boldly.

Consider the adverse effects of words!
An independent voice, as the human will decide,
The favor of expression as gifted, conferred
Accordingly, the discretion to individually exercise.
In life, even rights and freedoms bear a certain cost.
As such, should never be enjoyed at another's expense
That one even suffers needless injury or needless loss.
Such as is measured, in like measure, the consequence.

Writer's Block

To fall out with the mind is a terrible thing.
It is as if the mind has launched a defensive attack.
In such a case, it is virtually impossible to win
For the flow is interrupted by a mental block.
The lines of open communication are disrupted,
And as such, it results in a temporary shutdown.
And when the flow of information is interrupted,
All activities are halted; nothing else can be done.

The mind in fact has a mind of its own.
Like man does, the mind also lives and breathes.
And whenever confronted by a mental overload,
Self-preservation is its natural protective shield.
Whenever the needs of man become demanding,
In order to feed his insatiable hunger for growth,
Though driven yet lacking a real understanding,
The resulting effect could render the mind choked.

The mind is no doubt a terrible thing to waste.
It is very essential to the balance of the whole man.
With such a value, it is a loss that cannot be replaced.
Without it, it is impossible to independently stand.
Being creatively gifted by life is a divine gift of art.
Only those so blessed can fully appreciate its worth.
By its association with life, its expressions of thoughts,
Few gifts compare with the power of the spoken word.

But the mind, man's most precious gift of all,
Possesses its own sense of fear.
When broken and overwhelmed and in freefall,
It does as it must in accordance with its duty of care.
That bounty of riches; that unlimited power it holds!
He maintains the fate of life in the palms of his hands.
Hence the battleground which the enemy knows.
Whatever controls the mind controls the whole man.

Creatively gifted is such a blessing to be!
It holds an inner power which only few can appreciate.
But with such great power comes great accountability.
Considering man is the author and finisher of his fate,
His is a divine duty to preserve the integrity of his mind.
He must maintain its sense of balance at whatever the cost.
For an ill-fated fall from grace brought on by mental decline
Could lead man and mind to unrecoverable loss.

You

Imagine that unique and incomparable you!
Individual and distinct, you are unequaled to.
You are unlike any other, singular in identity.
An original thought, you were purposed to be
In a class all by yourself; you are one of a kind.
Not only special but extraordinary by design.

You are the author and finisher of your fate.
You are every decision that you willingly make.
Whatever the challenge that you may confront,
It is solely yours to decide to defeat or overcome.
The freedom to choose is a very powerful voice.
Even failing to choose is a passive choice.

You are whatever you do with each given day.
You are the mountain which stands in your way.
Whether surrender by retreat or a valiant dare,
You are your strongest motivator or greatest fear.
Nothing ever happens until or unless you move.
You are such as you have become, your attitude.

You are as your every embedded thought.
The power of imagination is what sets us apart.
Favored by creation, you were created by design.
The power is yours; become one with your mind.
While many have embraced the accepted limits,
You were favored with the gift of a creative spirit.

You are the direction of your personal growth.
You are an essential pillar in your own support.
Indeed, there are moments when life overwhelms,
But you are an agent of change; empower yourself!
The enemy is at the gate, and it is unrelenting too.
That which controls your mind also controls you.

Uniquely gifted, special, distinct, unequaled to—
Just a few of the many qualities embedded in you.
Favored by creation, you are bound by no set limits.
Among your abundance of favors is a creative spirit.
How life rewards you is totally dependent on you,
But nothing is going to move until or unless you do.

For the Good Times

If only but for the gift, and nothing else.
For the privilege of this very moment itself.
This amazing gift of the breath of life!
The joy of simply being alive!
Though it is not without its challenges,
Stilt, consider the freedom of choice it gives.
In spite of the ever-changing scenes of life;
There are still moments for which to smile—
For the good time.

If only but for the obstacles encountered,
For those times you contemplated surrender.
Yet, by seizing that one moment in time
You stood your ground and held the line.
Courage broke free, you confronted your fears;
The power of the mind became a valiant dare.
A new dawn breaks and with the sun, you rise.
You embrace the day with a victorious smile—
For the good times.

If only but for the power of a thought.
The still, small voice that ignited the spark.
Considering nothing ever moves until you do—
That the direction of growth depends on you.
Small wonder that the mind is the battle ground!
Man's most valued asset; his coveted crown.
But by the renewing of the spirit of the mind
Being in control you found a reason to smile—
For the good times.

If only but for it being a lifetime affair.
The expression of love, even the duty of care.
Celebrating personal victories, special moments—
The pillar of support when the heart was broken.
Battered by tumultuous storms, destructive waves—
Some by the forces of nature and others man made.
Though a journey of deep lows, yet uplifting highs.
Behind dark clouds, the silver lining still shines—
For the good times.

If only but for the measure of the man.
The joy of having the independent will to stand.
Enabled, that he might silence whatever the noise—
Empowered with the gift of the power of voice—
Being favored by creation, by a supernatural will
According to his need, life is duty bound to fulfil.
An elevated status, that he is the favor of life
The plain truth is reason enough to smile—
For the good times.

Foolish Advice

Consider this bit of foolish advice from me.
Day by day, you must train your eyes how to see.
And while you can't control what comes to your ears,
Be very tactful and selective of the things you hear.
In this arena you need to learn the art of survival.
The one you least expect may be your fiercest rival.

Along the pathways of life, it is important to learn
That there are unsuspecting snares at every turn.
Guard your tongue; it is the gateway to your heart.
While words build up, they also crudely tear apart.
Be mindful of your thoughts, they expose your soul.
Give away too much of yourself and you lose control.

The greatest teacher is not knowledge or experience,
Instead it is the application that makes the difference.
Stillness of the tongue is elevation for the wise
But the foolish suffers for ignoring sound advice.
As you make steady progress toward the mountain top,
Remember those you are going to meet on the way up.

Develop a thirst for knowledge as your lifelong quest.
Crave for it in like manner as your desire for success.
Image is nothing; it will not get you anywhere.
Approach and attitude will take you there.
Pay particular attention to life's little things,
There is an abundance of wealth concealed within.

Tell the winds in the plains of your personal cares.
Be ever mindful, hills have eyes and walls have ears.
Protect at all costs those things you value most,
Betrayal comes from within and it can alter a course.
Sometimes dialogue will suffice; no man is an island.
Do not let foolish pride destroy you where you stand.

An age-old principle: before honor comes humility.
The world is a global village; we are all one community.
Do not be fooled by appearances or the fallacy of fame,
There are undisclosed costs behind wealth and gains.
Develop your weaknesses and promote your strengths.
The greater your understanding, greater your confidence.

That man is the author and finisher of his own fate,
Be ever watchful, for at every turn evils lie in wait.
There are instances when it is wise to stoop to conquer—
To lose to win. Discretion is the better part of valor.
Above all else be true to yourself, live as you believe—
What a tangled web we weave when we practice to deceive!

Free Winded

Like the mighty wind is free, I wish I, too, can be!
That wherever I turn there is an open door.
All the world will be my playground to explore.
And, despite the mountains standing in my way,
As the morning sun, I rise like the light of day.
Like that spirited child knowing no sense of fear,
Oblivious to the dangers that lurk in the air,
The world and its myriad cares will be left behind.
Being free winded, such will be least on my mind.
No relationships of any sort, no lovers or friends,
Or personal obligations with which to contend.
With no burdens to bear or any measure of weight
At any given moment, I take to flight and escape.
I will have no pains of discomfort or fear being alone.
Even in the vacuum of space, I will still feel at home.
As healthy as ever, I will have no medical concerns.
No academic requirements or any skills to learn.
I will have no disturbing dreams or worry of death.
No actions in my past to look back at with regret.
Fearing no threat of violence or feuding enemies,
Being free winded I will soar wherever I please.
I could be the best of friend to the lonely at heart.
Or decide to clear clutter along life's beaten paths.
That overburdened soul, discouraged by despair—
Free winded, I can choose to offer a listening ear.
That tired and worn spirit at the end of a trying day—
I can become a wind of change and whisk it all away.
Today, I can choose to moonlight as a peaceful calm
Then at an instant, transform into a raging storm.
I will not be restricted by boundaries or dividing lines;

Nor any limitations, the discretion will be all mine.
No mountains will be too high or any distance too far.
I can play in the dirt and make my bed with the stars.
And with control of unlimited power at my fingertips
By the power which is vested in me, I do as I see fit.
I can excite the falling rains or provoke the quiet seas.
I can be as a gentle giant socializing with fallen leaves.
Those deeply buried, darkest secrets and hidden fears,
Even the whisper of a thought will be a breeze to hear.
I can go wherever I choose, whether by day or by night.
Even the mighty eagle can become my partner in flight.
I will answer only to he who entrusted this power to me.
Besides him, I will be subjected to no other authority.
I envy the wind! I wish I, too, can experience the same—
The freedom to enjoy the fullness of life, unrestrained.
Then, life would be as a breeze, stimulating within.
If only it were possible to live as free as the wind!

Free

Free! That is all I want to be.
Like the breath of life—
As an uninhibited smile—
Like the rising of the sun—
As the same going down—
All I want is to be free.
Free! That is all I want to be.
Like waves rushing ashore—
As their thunderous roars—
Like a bird on the winds—
As the wind beneath its wings—
All I want is to be free.
Free! That is all I want to be.
Like the spoken word—
As an expression unreserved—
Like the plant which grows—
As the water that flows—
All I want is to be free.
Free! That is all I want to be.
Like the falling rains—
As when seasons change—
Like the sound of music—
As the reaction to it—
All I want is to be free.
Free! That is all I want to be.
Like the roar of the ocean—
As energy in motion—
Like each beat of the heart—
As an expressed thought—
All I want is to be free.

Free! That is all I want to be.
Not by another's dictate,
Nor by any measured rate,
But as it is my right to be.
As does the whole, all of me.
All I want is to be free.

Freedom

If only but for the taste of freedom.
This life less wanted is weighing me down.
As the evil approaches, that which I loathe,
Vexing by nature, it fast tracks my growth.
Instead of chasing spirited winds in the wild
I bear the stature of a man in the body of a child.
Or being cradled in love, mine is a duty of care
Imposed, but for which I must be prepared.

If only but for the taste of freedom.
That which I fear most has finally come.
I am burdened with weight that I must bear;
A cloak of responsibility reserved, mine to wear.
Fate couldn't be unkinder or picked a worst day.
The joy of being a child is quietly vanishing away.
An untimely ascent into an established space.
Heredity is a line which time must never erase.

If only but for the taste of freedom.
I wish that this moment had never come.
A victim of circumstances; an unsettling state,
And, being next in line, no avenues of escape.
A new wind of change, sudden, without warning
Advancing in the distance as a new era dawns in.
The freedom I once knew has all but disappeared.
The lesson of the day, life is an adjustment affair.

If only but for the taste of freedom,
A moment longer before the evil days come
Ahead of the storm which is advancing my way.
Before I am overwhelmed by the evils of the day.
This cloak of responsibility I would rather not wear.
The weight on my shoulders I would rather not bear.
But if only for a moment longer, ahead of the storm,
Before the evil days come at the breaking of dawn.

If only but for the taste of freedom.
This elevation is an evil under the sun.
Instead of running with the winds as if wild
I am standing as a man in the body of a child.
This cloak of responsibility I would rather not wear.
This weight on my shoulders I would rather not bear.
I wish this day never ends and tomorrow never comes.
I would rather give it all if only for the taste of freedom.

I Rise

I have been tried by fire, tested to the core,
Brought down to lows I had never been before.
Frustrated by failures and intimidated by fears;
The agony of defeat surrounded me everywhere.
Felled without notice, faced unsettling setbacks;
Suffered losses, many came like sudden attacks.
Yet, despite the tempests, as tumults increased,
In the midst of the storms, I found my peace.
Behind the dark clouds, a light graced my eyes.
And as the light chased the shadows away, I rise.

I was wounded by words; felled to my knees.
The pains of discomfort exposed me with ease.
Shunned like a leper, an outcast, displaced,
Some within my circle withdrew from my face.
Betrayed, some of whom I held in high regard.
Bruised, to the extent I was extensively scarred.
And although some attacks left indelible stains
At the end of the day, the attempts were in vain.
Behind the dark clouds, a light graced my eyes.
And as the light chased the shadows away, I rise.

I lost my sense of balance, it rattled my mind,
Confused, I found myself behind enemy lines.
The agony of defeat stalked me like an easy prey;
The thrill of victory seemed a million miles away.
Frantic, in desperation I searched for a way out.
Behind enemy lines I was surrounded by doubt.
Yet, amid the confusion, I sensed a quieting calm.
Enter, an angel in waiting, an outstretched arm.
Behind the dark clouds, a light graced my eyes.

And as the light chased the shadows away, I rise.

I was created by design, by a supernatural will.
Unique, by intent, a particular purpose to fulfil.
I was gifted with the power of choice in my hands,
All of life before me, according to the master plan.
Nevertheless, I was blinded by the evils of the day.
I had gotten misdirected, my heart got in the way.
Fallen, bare and exposed, I lost my sense of place
Sill, love reached out to me with a warm embrace.
Behind the dark clouds, a light graced my eyes.
And as the light chased the shadows away, I rise.

War of Silence

Consider the destructive power of silence!
A passive resistance solely intent on defiance.
When communication falls in an offensive attack,
The thundery roars of silence defensively fire back.
A show of force is demonstrated as the tensions rise.
Defensive positions are reinforced on opposing sides.

A healthy relationship bursts as if a ruptured spleen.
A sudden explosion rattles an otherwise normal scene.
As emotions blind reason and tempers begin to flare,
The rift in communication results in a combative affair.
A misdirected ray of light converts into a lightning rod.
The spark ignites a fire, then the raising of the red flag.

With battle lines drawn, the engagement intensifies.
There seems no consideration or hope for compromise.
With neither party wavering, as the silence penetrates,
The state of affairs is worsened as conditions deteriorate.
And as both sides hold positions, claiming an advantage,
There is seemingly no thought given to collateral damage.

As the dispute rages on and tensions continue to rise,
A total disregard of costs over the failure to compromise.
As trust continually erodes and normal relations waver,
The lingering impasse tells of a costly falling out of favor.
A spark ignited a fire and then developed into open flames.
The winds excited the fury and spread it across the plains.

With boundaries clearly established and borders fortified,
The demarcation line that is drawn is the only compromise.
And, trapped deep in the middle, the most valued asset of all.
The ties that should forever bind are left tumbling in freefall.
And day after day, as tensions rise and the conflict lingers on,
The deafening silence thunders in the infuriated quiet storm.

The destructive power of silence! It ruptures the atmosphere.
An active, highly corrosive agent, it accelerates wear and tear.
For when emotions blind reason, communication takes the fall
And failing to find a middle ground, the imbalance affects all.
Silence may indeed be golden but never as a weapon of war,
For, at the cessation of hostilities, dead or alive, all bears scars.

Printed in the United States
By Bookmasters